BUSINESS *ENTERPRISE*

The
Small Business
Action Kit

REVISED FOURTH EDITION

John Rosthorn, Andrew Haldane,
Edward Blackwell and John Wholey

**Published in
association with**
**The Royal Bank
of Scotland**

**KOGAN
PAGE**

We would like to thank
Peter Allen for updating
this book in 1998

First published in 1986
Second edition 1988
Third edition 1991
© Macclesfield Business Ventures 1986, 1988, 1991

Fourth edition 1994, reprinted with revisions 1995
© Kogan Page Ltd 1994
Reprinted with revisions 1998

Kogan Page Limited
120 Pentonville Road
London N1 9JN

British Library Cataloguing in Publication Data

A CIP record for this book is available from the British Library.

ISBN 0–7494–1257–7

Typeset by Books Unlimited (Nottm), Sutton-in-Ashfield, NG17 1AL
Printed and bound in Great Britain by Biddles Ltd, Guildford and King's Lynn

◀ CONTENTS ▶

◄ CHAPTER 1 ►

AM I UP TO RUNNING MY OWN BUSINESS?

Introduction

For most adults, there are but three options where work is concerned:
unemployment, employment and self-employment.

Unemployment	
Advantages	*Disadvantages*

Employment	
Advantages	*Disadvantages*

Self-employment	
Advantages	*Disadvantages*

Using the grids on page 9, rule up a sheet of paper and write down the advantages and disadvantages of each in your own circumstances.

This book is mainly concerned with the successful establishment and expansion of self-employment which will in turn provide employment opportunities for others.

Ideas for business

Think about what you can do

While there are a few 'ideas' magazines and consultants around, most would-be businesspeople have to think up the ideas that would suit them.

Business ideas may be generated through two routes, inspirational and analytical.

1. Inspirational

- A gap in the market-place not satisfied by existing suppliers.
- A new solution to an existing problem; an invention, a process or method.

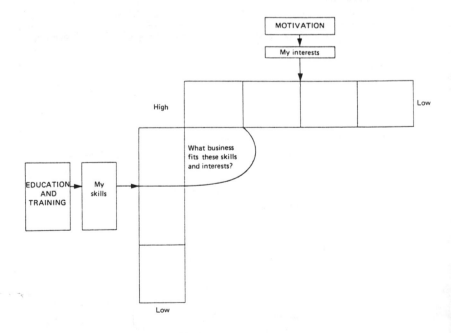

2. Analytical

Write *your* high interest and high skills factors in the boxes provided.

What businesses match your high scores?

The seven stages of business start-up

These seven points are designed to help you find where you are, and therefore to see what remains to be done.

What needs to be done

At which stage are you?

Tick box when stage is completed.

1. *Acquiring motivation.* Finding the urge and energy to pursue the goal of setting up a business. Checking your own personal capability. *Do you have what it takes?* ☐

2. *Finding an idea* which it seems reasonable to spend *time* and *money* on taking further. ☐

3. *Proving the idea.* Design and manufacture of samples. Testing the product/service technically and with customers. Testing the market. Understanding the market. Protecting the product/ service by patents and registered design. ☐

4. *Knowing what is needed.* Developing the framework for getting into business: ☐
   - Premises, cash, equipment, labour.
   - The time needed to assemble all the resources.
   - Adequate quality control.
   - Professional help in starting a business plan (see page 80).

5. *Under starter's orders.* Applying the business plan. Negotiating for finance, premises, contracts, subcontracts etc. Choosing business name, brand names, the structure (type of company) and registering them. Tax considerations. Use of professional advisers. Getting the right staff. Preparing publicity. ☐

6. *The 'off'*. First manufacture, first sale. Launch publicity.

7. *Staying the course.* Keeping track of results. Compare with business plan. Keeping a grip on things. Organising the work. Watching for changes in the market and the law. Keeping the workforce, customers and suppliers happy. Anticipating snags. Improving the product. Looking at competitors.

Note carefully how much more still remains to be done.

Personal preparation

Complete this checklist

While this checklist is designed to encourage new business start-ups, it also highlights areas where you are apparently ill-equipped. Check your answers with your spouse and your business partner.

Yes or No

1. Are your physical health and age compatible with your proposed project?

2. Can you cope mentally with the new stresses and demands?

3. Do you welcome:
   - calculated risks?
   - responsibility?

4. Have you demonstrated management ability?

5. Do you have the quality of endurance?

6. Can you work alone for sustained periods?

7. Can you accept a reduced income?

8. Will you work without normal financial security?

9. Are you self-confident in the face of adversity and rebuffs?

10. Do you know how many hours per week you wish to work?

Yes or No

11. Do you know how supportive your wife/husband will be? ☐

12. Have you discussed the project with: ☐
    • her/him?
    • the children?

13. Do you appreciate what effect it could have on: ☐
    • family life?
    • the family home?
    • other assets?

14. Have you listed your personal skills? ☐

15. Do you know the business you are going into well? ☐

16. Can you identify what your business project will need from you? ☐

17. Do you know why you want to start the project? ☐

18. Have you set out truthfully what you want out of the business, ☐
    and when?

19. Will your project affect your personality? ☐

20. Do you know what your attitude is towards ☐
    • paying taxes?
    • long working hours?
    • selling?
    • asking for money?
    • asking for help?
    • power?
    • success?
    • failure?

21. Are there religious, social, educational or ethical limitations on ☐
    your business performance?

22. Can you take decisions? ☐

Yes or No

23. Do you get on with people? ☐

24. Have your realistically listed your personal attributes and shortcomings? ☐

25. Will you discuss this listing with an honest and respected friend? ☐

Press on to the next stage of the project if you have truthfully answered 'Yes' to almost every question.

If most of your answers are 'No', perhaps you should think again about trying to start your own business.

Initial preparation for the business

How knowledgeable are you? Now to the business itself. How much do you know about your business area? Use this checklist:

Yes or No

1. Do you have a clear idea of the business opportunity now facing you? ☐

2. Will your product sell? ☐

3. Do you accurately understand your intended product/service? ☐

4. Have you looked at the market for it? ☐
   - What people buy
   - When they buy it
   - Where they buy it
   - Who does the buying
   - Why they should choose your product/service
   - How you will set about selling your product/service
   - How big the market is for your product
   - Whether it will grow or contract
   - What your share of the market will be

Yes or No

5. Have you checked the moral, legal and environmental objections to your project? ☐

6. Do you know why your product is best? ☐

7. Can you explain this clearly to customers? ☐

8. Will it remain the best? ☐

9. Does it do what you say it does; has it been tested? ☐

10. Will you continue to improve your product? ☐

11. Do you know where new products will come from? ☐

12. Have you sold your product yet? ☐

13. Are you familiar with what customers want? ☐
    - Delivery and after-sales service requirements
    - Quality levels
    - Discount levels

14. Do you know who your competitors are? ☐

15. Do you know what they will do if you enjoy some success? ☐

16. Can you keep up to date with changing techniques and technology? ☐

17. Have you spoken to any potential customers about the market? ☐

18. Do you know what your product will cost to make? ☐

19. Have you calculated your overheads, including selling and distribution? ☐

20. Have you attempted a simple cash flow projection? ☐

21. At this stage do you have an idea of:
    * How much cash you will need in the next 12 months?
    * How much cash you can personally raise?
    * How much external cash you need?
    * When you can repay it?

22. Have you agreed within the family what security you can offer your financiers?

23. Do your partners/shareholders understand your project?

24. Do you know how much it will cost to publicise your product?

25. Do you have:
    * A solicitor?
    * An accountant?
    * A bank manager?
    * Other essential specialists?

26. Have these specialists been properly briefed about the services you require and replied formally about the cost of the service?

27. Have you identified the problems you have never faced before?

The first phase of setting up in business is only completed when you have truthfully answered 'Yes' to virtually all these questions.

Cost of living

Your living expenses

	Current annual expenses	Economics which can be sustained for a time	Economics which can be made for a lengthy period
Rent or mortgage payments			
Council tax			
Food			
Heating, lighting, water			
House repairs/maintenance			
Personal travel			
Vehicle repairs/maintenance			
Insurances			
Holidays and entertainment			
Clothing			
Subscriptions			
Gifts			
Others —			
—			
—			
TOTAL	£	£	£

Now, how much do you need to earn gross from your business, before income tax and National Insurance?

- Per month £
- Per annum £

Personal and domestic costs have a real bearing on the required financial return from a business venture. Fill in the table and work out how much you will need to earn to pay your way.

The final test

Your professional capabilities

How well do you understand the following and does your business plan cover them adequately?

- Business finance
- Principal risks to your business
- The competition you will face
- General management of a business
- Marketing
- Production (if applicable)

How strong is your own record of achievement in industry or commerce?

Unless a realistic assessment of your capabilities gives satisfactory answers to these questions, there are two possible courses of action:

1. Abandon the idea.

2. Take steps to correct weak areas *before* starting the business. For example:
    - Enrol on a relevant 'Start a Business' course
    - Engage qualified professional advisers
    - Find partners/shareholders/employees with the required experience
    - Ask your bank for all the literature it has on how to start and run a small business.

◄ CHAPTER 2 ►

WHAT ARE THE OPTIONS?

Business start-ups

There is a very limited number of ways of getting into business.

Which best meets the constraints you have in terms of skills, experience, money, property? Does your preferred choice really offer you a future?

What about the others?

Ways of getting into business

1. Buy an existing business
2. Buy the assets of a failed business
3. Put together a new business

    (a) Similar to what is already being done
    (b) Novel or unique product/service

4. Take up a franchise (see page 24).

In your situation	
Advantages	*Disadvantages*

Buying a business

Buying an existing business avoids having to start from scratch

The ways in which businesses may be acquired are few in number. This chart sets out the major issues upon which professional advice should taken to minimise the risk of loss or unnecessary expense.

Purchaser	Vendor	Method
Individual, partnership or company	Sole trader, partnership or company	Acquire assets

Watch out for these points

- Valuation of fixed assets and stock
- Valuation of goodwill (ie the difference between the asking price for the business and the value of its physical assets)
- Some assets may not be legally transferable
- Transfer of patents, trade marks, licences, copyright and other assets
- Service contracts
- Vendor responsible for redundancies
- Freedom of 'old' management to set up in competition

Purchaser	Vendor	Method
Individual or partnership	Shareholders	Acquire shares

Watch out for these points
Acquired as a going concern, hence:

- Product liability for old defaults
- Existing contracts maintained including employment
- Pension liabilities taken over
- Obtain warranties and indemnities from vendor
- Liability for debts if trading when insolvent
- Control exercised through shareholders*

* A majority shareholding exceeding 50 per cent gives day-to-day control of a company subject to the law of the land and contractual obligations entered into. But some important purposes – notably winding up the company – may require a 75 per cent interest.

Purchaser	Vendor	Method
Company	Shareholders	Acquire shares – for cash – by issue of shares

Watch out for these points
As above for individual or partnerships, *plus*
Consolidation of group accounts

In an open market, a business is worth what the highest bidder will pay for it. It does not follow that this price is fair, right or moral. LOOK OUT!

Buying a shop

Because Britain is alleged to be a 'nation of shopkeepers', and because most shops fail, it is particularly necessary to question your plans.

Retailing is the most popular field on which people start up

1. Why do you want to buy a shop? Name your reasons.

2. What direct competition exists in the area?

3. What indirect competition is there?
   • Mail order
   • Party plan
   • Fairs
   • Markets

4. In the catchment area, what is the:
   • Population?
   • Unemployment level?
   • Purchasing power?

And their trends?

What effect might recent or likely changes in these trends have on the business?

5. Is the area to be redeveloped?
   (a) Any supermarkets proposed? Will these compete?
   (b) Any road widening or change of traffic flows proposed? Will these affect the business?
   (c) Will the proximity of suppliers change? With what effect?

6. What are, or will be, the main customer types, eg school children for shops near to schools? Any changes likely?

7. How many people pass the shop each day?

   What proportion of them want your intended product range?

   What will be the size of the average purchase?

8. Walk the streets. Talk to neighbouring shopkeepers, customers and your bank's local manager. Read the local newspapers. Find out all you can about trade in the street and the locality.

9. Note dates of ownership of:

Current owner	19XX – 19XX	Why is he/she selling?
Prior owner	19XX – 19XX	

   What does this information indicate?

10. What are current:

Sales	£	/week
Purchases	£	/week
Gross margins by product		per cent

    Check till rolls.

    Check paying-in books, purchase invoices and delivery notes.

    Ignore stories of 'cash into the back pocket'.

11. Check what the professionally prepared accounts indicate about:

		This year	Last year	Prior year
Sales	£			
Expenses	£			
Profits	£			

Now do your own forecasts.

12. Check rate of staff turnover. How many will stay on with the new owner?
    Can you recruit new staff successfully?

13. Have comparisons with other shops and businesses been made?

14. What would be the value of the freehold or the lease if property were empty?

15. How much will you need to borrow? £
    Will the business support this borrowing?

16. Have you organised advice from accountants, valuers, solicitors?

17. What hours will you have to work?

    Calculate $\dfrac{\text{Profit}}{\text{Your annual working hours}} = £ \ /\text{hour}$

18. Note living accommodation, proximity of schools and churches, recreation facilities, car parks, transport and other social factors.

19. See question 1. Do you still want to buy this shop?
    If so, write down why.

Also do the calculations on page 24.

Current income versus self-employment

Will you be better off financially if you go into business on your own account?

It is easy to suppose that self-employment will bring greater income – it rarely does! Try this exercise to see how your project looks.

A	Enter purchase price of business (excluding stock).	£
B	Enter stock as valued.	£
C	Enter cost of improvements needed, if any.	£
D	Enter any other costs, eg legal fees etc.	£
E	Add A,B,C and D together = Total cost of business.	£
F	Enter *net* profit (pre-tax) including any proprietor's salary in last year of business, but be sure you have deducted the bank or loan interest *you* will have to pay.	£
G	Enter *net* profit (pre-tax) estimated for *next* year including proprietor's salary, but be sure you have deducted the bank or loan interest *you* will have to pay.	£
H	Enter current interest paid on present cash on deposit or other investments to be sold.	£
I	Enter your present annual earnings or social security payments.	£
J	Add H and I together.	£
K	Deduct J from F = Benefit from running business (calculated on current earnings).	£
L	K ÷ E × 100 = Return on investment (calculated on current earnings).	%
M	Deduct J from G = Benefit from running business (calculated on estimated earnings).	£
N	M ÷ E × 100 = Return on investment (calculated on estimated future earnings).	%

There are other valid reasons for starting a business. What are yours?

But don't forget these figures.

One option: taking up a franchise

Franchises offer a ready-made business formula with constant support from the franchisor.

Franchises are growing rapidly. In the UK there have been some remarkable success stories, eg Body Shop and Dyno-Rod. Franchises have continued to increase in importance as opportunities for new business start-ups. Because they have a much higher survival rate, they are viewed favourably by outside investors, notably the banks.

Setting up a franchise

The franchisor will eventually sell a package of *proven* know-how relating to a specific type of business activity. With the package, the franchisor is likely to attract sound franchisees and the necessary finance. The franchisor will have to complete the following steps prior to launching a programme:

1. Eliminate as soon as possible the risks inherent in any business start-up by thoroughly market testing a small number of pilot operations.

   The franchise package

2. Provide the means by which the franchisee can be his/her own boss.

3. Develop a detailed operational manual setting out how the business should be run.

4. Develop strong branding of the franchise through media appropriate to the franchise's target market.

5. Prepare the franchise prospectus to show anticipated returns on investment.

6. Obtain Newspaper Publishers Association approval prior to advertising for franchisees, although this is probably dealt with through the publication in which the franchisor chooses to advertise the scheme.

7. Protect intellectual property: patents, trade marks, copyrights.

8. Prepare the franchise agreement with a solicitor experienced in this field.

9. Obtain in-principle support from the franchise specialist units in the major banks.

10. Consider joining the British Franchise Association: Thames View, Newtown Road, Henley-on-Thames, Oxon RG9 1HG; telephone 01491 578049.

Franchisee's checklist

1. *Check out the business environment*   *Tick when checked*
   - (a) Analyse own motivation and capabilities. ☐
   - (b) Review commitment of the immediate family to the idea. ☐
   - (c) Assess public awareness and acceptability of franchised product. ☐
   - (d) Check protection of product by patents, trade marks, copyrights. ☐
   - (e) Look for strong possibility of expanded use of product. ☐
   - (f) Review strength of competition, franchised or otherwise. ☐
   - (g) Examine pricing. ☐

2. *Check out the franchisor*
   - (a) Find out length of time and experience in franchising in the UK. ☐
   - (b) Obtain the bank status report and latest audited accounts. ☐
   - (c) Look at the management structure. ☐
   - (d) Review communication systems and effectiveness. ☐
   - (e) Contact other existing franchisees. ☐
   - (f) Get comments on operations manual. ☐
   - (g) Note payments to franchisor: fee, royalty, levy. ☐

3. *Check the franchise agreement*
   - (a) Note terms and conditions of renewal. ☐
   - (b) Look at franchisor's and franchisee's obligations. ☐
   - (c) Check out franchisor's accountability regarding advertising and other levies. ☐
   - (d) Examine franchise sale options. ☐
   - (e) Note minimum sales quantity requirement and other termination clauses. ☐
   - (f) Understand exclusivity of territories. ☐
   - (g) Note compulsory death and incapacity covers. ☐
   - (h) Note VAT liabilities on fees, royalties etc. ☐

◀ CHAPTER 3 ▶

WHAT HAS TO BE DONE? WHO WILL HELP?

Countdown to start-up

This list outlines matters to be resolved before a business can start trading. Use the boxes to indicate what you have completed.

	Date done	See also page	Check whether you have dealt with these matters

1. Note the addresses and phone numbers of local business advisers such as:
   - Small Firms Service ☐
   - Rural Development Commission ☐
   - Small Business Club ☐
   Check availability of local courses on starting a business ☐ 39–41
2. Research and understand the market for your product. ☐
3. Establish preliminary product costings. ☐ 123–5
4. Review the qualifications for the Business Start-up Allowance (Jobcentre leaflet). If appropriate, book in for an 'information session' through the Jobcentre. *Don't* start trading until accepted on to the scheme, if you are eligible. ☐
5. Appoint your accountant; agree service and fee. Establish business records systems. ☐ 31

	Date done	*See also page*

6. Appoint your solicitor; agree service and fee. Review the form of your business. ☐ 31–2

7. Select business name. ☐ 106

8. Find and cost premises. Consult Fire Brigade about expenses associated with obtaining a Fire Certificate. ☐ 92–3, 97

9. Check with Planning Office, District or Borough Council, about planning and building regulations constraints on the property/home. Note restrictions on the use of advertising signs. ☐ 91, 98–102

10. Advise your bank manager of your plans. ☐ 32

11. Determine what licences, certificates etc will be necessary to permit you to trade. ☐ 110, 111

12. Investigate patent, registered design, trade mark and copyright protection. Apply for protection if justifiable. ☐ 113–15

13. Check the availability of grant aid for your business. ☐ 88–90

14. Locate key suppliers, confirm their prices and deliveries. ☐ 119–20

15. Establish your prices and discounts. ☐ 43–6

16. Complete the business plan, including 12-month financial plan.
    NB Ensure business plan includes sufficient cash being available to cover the requirement of the first 12 months. ☐ 80–82

17. Obtain from bank written confirmation of loan/overdraft facilities. Seek to understand how arrangement fees, bank charges and interest will be charged. Open the bank account. ☐ 76, 86–8

18. If applicable, form a company or draw up a partnership agreement. ☐ 103–8

19. For business premises, take professional advice on leases, purchase and licences. ☐ 31–3, 94

20. Apply for and obtain permission to trade where necessary (see also 11 above). ☐ 98, 100

21. Inform Inspector of Taxes that you are starting in business, preferably through your accountant, using Form 41G. Provide him with your P45. Read booklet IR28 'Setting Up in Business'. ☐ 109

Date done   *See also*
                page

22. Inform Department of Social Security (DSS) for National Insurance purposes. Check availability of Income Support. ☐

23. Establish income tax and National Insurance contribution deductions using appropriate forms. Be familiar with Statutory Sick Pay (SSP) Scheme and Statutory Maternity Pay (SMP). ☐

24. Contact VAT Office and, if necessary, establish records and registration (in telephone directory under Customs and Excise). ☐

25. Confirm mail and telephone links with Post Office and British Telecom. ☐

26. Plan communications of product/service to your target market. ☐

27. Make sure appropriate insurance covers are taken out. ☐

28. Establish terms and conditions of employment. Note the requirement to maintain existing terms and conditions where an existing business is being taken over. ☐

29. Contact Jobcentre regarding future employees. ☐

30. Take delivery of all business stationery and promotional materials. ☐

31. Advise the Rating Department of your local council. Check payment options. Avoid paying rates on empty premises. If you live on your business premises there may be liability for both council tax and business rates. ☐

32. Factories: advise Health and Safety Executive. ☐

33. Shops and offices: complete and return Form OSR 1 to Environmental Health and Housing Department, District or Borough Council. ☐

34. Ensure mains services are connected to your premises:
    - Gas ☐
    - Electricity (single/three phase) ☐
    - Water ☐
    - Drainage ☐

35. For credit or hire sales, apply to Trading Standards Office. ☐

	Date done	*See also page*

36. Prepare launch of the business with press/media support. ☐ 47–56
37. Take out bank and credit references for major new, unknown credit customers. Think twice about some known credit customers. ☐ 126
38. Consider joining the:
    - Small Business Club ☐
    - Chamber of Commerce, or equivalent ☐
    - Chamber of Trade ☐
    - Trade Association, eg Master Builders, Licensed Victuallers. ☐

Selection of professional advisers

All small businesses should seek cost-effective contributions to the management of their business from appropriate professional advisers. Key professions include accountants, solicitors, estate agents and bank managers.

The best times to make the choice are:

- before the business begins operations
- before a new phase in the development of the business.

The steps in the selection process are:

1. Make appointments and visit at least two, preferably three, of each class of adviser.
2. Discuss your business opportunity. Agree with the adviser the list of services he/she can provide to meet business needs.
3. Agree the dates by which the services will be provided.
4. Discuss the cost of the service and the terms of payment for it.
5. Obtain confirmation in writing of points 2, 3 and 4.
6. Make your selection on the basis of the written confirmation and the personal interview.
7. Courteously advise the prospective advisers of your choice.

Services available from your advisers.

The checklists will help you to see what your advisers can do for you. It is your job to ensure that you get value for money spent on buying their services.

Check what various advisers can offer

Accountant

Your accountant should be a vital member of your small management team.

Accountant

- Company formation
- Partnership agreements
- Accounting/Bookkeeping systems
- Value Added Tax (VAT)
- Pay As You Earn (PAYE)/National Insurance administration
- Government grants
- Business planning including budgets and forecasts
- Cash raising
- Management information
- Interim accounts preparation
- Year-end accounts preparation
- Annual audit
- Capital restructuring
- Business tax
- Business tax planning
- Company secretarial services
- Personal tax
- Personal tax planning
- Pension arrangements/schemes
- Disability arrangements
- Death cover
- Retirement planning
- Investment planning
- Inheritance Tax planning
- Wills
- Receiverships and liquidations

Solicitor

Your solicitor will prove to be of vital importance on occasions during the formation, growth and, perhaps, the winding up of your business. Agree the service(s) to be provided.

Solicitor

- Tailor-made company formation and registration
- Partnership agreements. A written agreement covering basic terms is advisable.
- Property – freehold and lease negotiations and conveyancing
- Employment law, eg contracts of employment
- Commercial law, eg agency appointments
- Debt collection
- Inter-company disputes
- Distribution, licensing, secrecy, manufacturing agreements
- Patents and copyright
- Terms of trade
- Personal guarantees.

Bank

Bank

Your bank is a very necessary part of your business from the start. A vast organisation of specialists is available to guide you in the financial planning of your business, and on the best use of funds.

A short guide to possible facilities available:

- *Current account.* For day-to-day trading.
- *Deposit account.* For investment of surplus funds – special rates for larger deposits.
- *Loan account* (long term). Capital borrowings repaid over period of years.
- *Assistance in importing and exporting.* Advice on methods, finance; economic intelligence reports on countries worldwide.
- *Provision of finance.* Overdraft, loans, discounting, bills of exchange, medium-term loans, business start-up loans, business expansion loans, government Loan Guarantee Scheme.
- *Leasing/factoring services.* Through specialist bank subsidiaries.
- *Transmission of funds.* Credit transfers, overseas payments, direct debit system etc.

Your local manager is available to give on-the-spot advice in all matters relating to the financial aspect of your business.

Architect

Architect

Your architect is a valuable member of the building team in the construction of new premises and the alteration of existing buildings.

An architect's work includes site investigation, feasibility studies, obtaining planning consents, investigation into problems of strength, construction, weather proofing, energy conservation etc.

An architect knows the best way through all the problems and regulations associated with building, and will look after your interests through all or any stages of a building project.

Services supplied by your architect may include:

- *New buildings.* Investigation of site, town planning problems, feasibility studies including estimates of the cost of the project, sketch plans, working drawings, obtaining competitive quotations, preparing contracts, supervising the work to completion.
- *Old buildings.* In addition to the services listed above for new buildings, your architect may be able to complete feasibility studies regarding alterations and improvements.
- *Grant work.* Advising on any grants available.
- *Litigation.* Providing technical expertise in building dispute cases.
- *Energy saving.* Advising on economies in heating of properties and on any grants and other such help available to meet the costs of new installations to achieve energy saving.
- *Advice on leases on purchase of property.* Advice can be given on the conditions attached to purchases on leases, including the preparation of schedules of conditions to be incorporated in any lease.

Surveyor and most estate agents

Where bank lending is to finance the purchase of a property, the bank will require a valuation of that property by a reputable valuation surveyor. Sometimes banks recommend a valuer; others let you choose your own. If you choose your own, advise the bank of your choice at an early stage. Always choose a member of the Royal Institution of Chartered Surveyors (RICS) or the Incorporated Society of Valuers and Auctioneers (ISVA). **Surveyor/Estate agent**

The surveyor will also be able to advise on the following:

If you are buying:

- Structural condition of the property

- Whether or not the rating assessment is too high
- Defective workmanship
- Whether or not planning permission is required and making the application.

If you are leasing:

- The condition of the property and make recommendations. Modern leases usually make the tenant responsible for all repairs; with older buildings the implications can be immense. A surveyor will advise on schedules of condition and negotiate your lease terms.
- Rating
- Planning permission
- Negotiating the rent at the commencement of the lease or upon rent review.

The surveyor will also be able to recommend members of other associated professions who can give more detailed advice on heating, electrical installations and building design.

Insurance adviser

Insurance adviser

Your insurance adviser is important at all stages of your business career, from initial planning onwards. He will help you to ensure the continuation of your business and your income should accidents occur, and also ensure that you meet any legal requirements, eg public liability insurance.

Certain areas of insurance such as life and pensions require a specialist adviser.

When you seek his advice you should cover the areas listed below. Choose an adviser who is helpful, efficient and trustworthy.

- *General*
  Accident, fire, theft, vehicles, stock, equipment etc
- *Business*
  Liability and consequential loss
- *Sickness*
  Personal accident, temporary/permanent disability, private medical care

- *Death*
  Of key personnel, shareholder, owner or partner
- *Pension*
  Directors, employers, employees
  State, insured and self-administered schemes
- *Loans*
  Alongside pension or pension loanback
- *Personal investment planning*
  Your capital and/or income requirements or aims outside direct business growth.

If the insurance covers are to be arranged through a broker, be sure to enquire about the insurance company with which the business is placed.

Design consultant

Design has a vital, often misunderstood, role in improving profitability.   **Design consultant**

Ask yourself the following questions:

1. Will improved design increase my share of the intended, or existing, market?
2. Will it reduce manufacturing costs?
3. Will it improve the product?
4. Will it improve cash flow, net of costs?

Where the answer is 'Yes' to these questions, contact a designer, looking for these particular points:

(a) Designer should spend enough time learning about you and your business.
(b) Obtain a 'no obligation' proposal of design work founded on the areas already agreed in discussions.
(c) Ensure your designer submits the proposal accurately describing work to be undertaken, in stages, with time and costs clearly shown.
(d) Brilliance is no substitute for experience, so choose a designer with a track record. Ask for references; discover whether the design experience is suitable to your need.

Then:
(e) Payment should be made only after the satisfactory completion of each stage.

Design assistance may be available under the Design Initiative of the Department of Trade and Industry, information about which is given in a booklet, available by telephoning 0800 500 200, and entitled 'The Enterprise Initiative'.

Public relations consultant

PR consultant

The PR task is to help you devise your company message, to select who receives it, and to make sure that you communicate that company message to the target group in the outside world.

- *Press releases*
  The most common form of PR. Prepare your message, usually in the form of a press release about your product, despatch to the relevant media (newspapers, magazines, trade journals, radio or TV); could involve a press reception or special events to attract media attention.
- *Corporate PR*
  Will help you to describe your company to the outside world: could take the form of a company brochure, film or video; may involve research into how other people (eg your suppliers or customers) see you and how to change their views (or yours) for the better.
- *Lobbying*
  Is intended to change the view of a legislative body (eg Parliament, EC committees, the Town Hall), by preparing a case for their consideration. Methods include: arranging special meetings, personal contact, public exposure.
- *Financial PR*
  Is intended to attract investors to your company. Work with brokers and merchant banks to ensure the correct company profile or to attract attention in the specialist financial media.
- *Industrial PR*
  Helps you to explain company activities to your employees. It can take the form of a company newsletter, open days, sponsorship of sports teams or local events.

PR for new companies

A new company needs to identify its 'publics'. Who would influence the success of your business? Is it the Town Hall, the local residents, employees, an untapped market, a trade union or a government department?

PR consultancies can help you with a wide variety of marketing and management tasks. Larger companies employ specialists in market research, audio-visual production, management consultancy, promotions and advertising, but a smaller company can get this advice from their PR consultancy. Writing customer letters, sales leaflets or video scripts, for example, is often the area where a PR consultancy is particularly helpful.

Advertising agent

It is probably more important for a small firm to make effective use of its promotional funds than it is for a large company. A well-chosen and well-briefed advertising agency can make a big contribution to this work.

Advertising agent

A 'full service' advertising agency will handle:

- *Research.* Market, advertising, pricing, pack
- *Campaign presentation.* Artwork, layout, copy, media, design
- *Implementation.* Production, media buying, delivery, insertions, monitoring of costs and effectiveness
- *Sales promotion.* Pack, deals
- *Merchandising/Display.* Point of sale work
- *Development.* Product, market
- *Forecasting.* Sales, mathematical modelling
- *Exhibitions.* Stand design and management
- *Public relations.* Media, lobbying.

Smaller agencies may handle just one or two of the functions listed.

The small business client should approach his briefing of the advertising on the basis of:

- Knowing the *product benefits*
- Knowing the *target market* – the customer
- Knowing what the advertising must do.

Dealing with your local council

Your local council

Executives or officials employed by the council have delegated powers enabling them to take decisions which may affect your business. In other cases the powers are retained by sub-committees or the council itself, which may accept or reject advice provided by the officers. To benefit your business you should know who takes the decision and how. Contact your local council to find out which committee decides what.

◄ CHAPTER 4 ►

NO CUSTOMERS – NO BUSINESS

Market research for the small business

Whatever your talents are as a skilled craftsperson, top executive, butcher, baker or candlestick maker, all have one thing in common – *no customers, no business.* A vague idea that there are lots of people out there who need me is a pleasant thought and good for the ego – but it won't pay the rent, and it won't convince your bank manager to lend you money.

Market research is essential to gain a thorough knowledge of your customers and competitors

The way to understand better whether customers truly exist is to ask the right questions:

1. How many *potential customers are there?*
2. *How many real* customers are there?
3. Who are they?
4. Who does the buying?
5. Where is the buying done?
6. Where are the customers?
7. What kind of product or service do they want to buy?
8. Why do they want the product or service?
9. Where do they get it at present?
10. How much will they want to pay?
11. What deficiencies do the current products or services have?
12. When do customers buy, how much and how frequently?
13. Can you deliver what they want when they want it?
14. Who else can supply this product/service?

15. How strong is this competition?
16. Will the market grow or contract?

The answers to questions may be found by:

(a)   *'Desk' research.* Newspapers, advertisements, libraries, reference works, textbooks, market surveys.
(b)   *Visiting potential retailers/distributors.* Talking to them in a pre-planned way, finding out prices and discounts.
(c)   *Visiting competitors.* Talking to them, obtaining literature, price-lists and samples.
(d)   *Observing similar establishments.* Customer flow.
(e)   *Visiting users.* Discussing what benefits they associate with your product or product type.

Such contacts may be made by:

- Personal visit – the best.
- Telephone – but only by a skilled person aided by a written guideline.
- Mail questionnaire – but expect a low response.

Part of the market research is quite properly descriptive – 'feel' – and is described as *qualitative* research. For analysts such as bank managers and business advisers, there is also a vital requirement for numbers: *quantitative* research.

For would-be retailers, traffic flow into the shop is vital. Research location!

Sources of market information

Sources of
information

In the preparation for the business start-up, it can be easy to neglect the opportunity to check published information – often available free of charge – which may allow the market size, trends, prices and customers to be identified.

Agricultural Statistics, HMSO
Annual Abstract of Statistics, HMSO
Census of Population, HMSO

County, borough and town profiles, county and district councils (various)
Digest of UK Energy Statistics, HMSO
Dun & Bradstreet Directories
Employment Gazette, HMSO
European Marketing Data and Statistics, Euromonitor
Family Expenditure Survey, HMSO
Financial Statistics, HMSO
General Household Survey, HMSO
Inland Revenue Statistics, HMSO
Kelly's Business Directory, Kelly's Directories
Kompass Register, Kompass Publishers
Main Economic Indicators, HMSO
Market Research Great Britain, Euromonitor
Mintel Market Intelligence, Mintel
National Income and Expenditure, HMSO
Regional Trends, HMSO
Social Trends, HMSO
Thomson Directory
Yellow Pages

Have you visited your local library? Much of this information and more is waiting for you there.

Product pricing

Avoiding the temptation to establish prices on the basis of internal costs, the successful business:

The question of pricing

1. Researches prices and discounts in the market
2. Remembers that price is an attribute of the market *and* product or service
3. Assesses other elements in the competition – notably quality and delivery
4. Knows that it is easier to reduce a price than to put it up.

For a conventional manufactured product sold by wholesale and retail distribution, this price schedule may help you to price your product in the market-place.

	Main competitors									Your product	
	1			2			3			Initial price	Adjusted price
	Pack size			Pack size			Pack size				
	A	B	C	A	B	C	A	B	C		
Name of product											
Main retailer											
Recommended retail price											
Marketed price											
Actual selling price											
Trade price* Volume discounts											
Net trade price*											
Wholesale price* Volume discounts											
Net wholesale price*											
Quality rating											
Delivery rating											
Other ratings											

* It may be difficult to get all this information.

Price as an attribute of the product or service

It is too easy, and bad business, to think that the new product or service has to be the cheapest.

Compare your product or service with those of your competitors

This table encourages you to compare your products with your competitors'. Tick as appropriate.

Comparison with competitors

Product attributes	Worse -3 -2 -1	Same 0	Better +1 +2 +3	Is attribute important to the customer? Tick
Design				
Performance				
Packaging				
Presentation/appearance				
After-sales service				
Availability				
Delivery				
Colour/flavour/ odour/touch				
Image				
Specification				
Payment terms				
Others:				

Now look again at:

Discounts

Price

43

Discounts and price changes

Discounts

Suppliers may offer cash discounts for prompt payment of outstanding bills. Use this table to see how the cost of the deal compares with overdraft or loan interest rates.

Discount forgone: %	Annual interest rate % to break even (pre-tax) (Cost in %) Extra credit taken – in weeks								
	5	6	7	8	9	10	11	12
1	10.5	8.7	7.5	6.6	5.8	5.2	4.8	4.4
1½	15.8	13.1	11.3	9.9	8.8	7.9	7.2	6.6
2	21.1	17.6	15.1	13.2	11.7	10.5	9.6	8.8
2½	26.4	22.0	18.9	16.5	14.7	13.2	12.0	11.0
3	31.8	26.5	22.7	19.9	17.7	15.9	14.4	13.2
5	53.5	44.6	38.2	33.5	29.7	26.8	24.3	22.3

Price reductions

Cut the price to increase sales volume. Before you do, check that the sales volume increase needed to break even (ignoring the costs of handling increased sales volumes) really will happen. Beware of setting off a price war with your competitors; it is the route to ruin for you all.

	Percentage sales volume increase needed to break even on a price reduction						
	Gross margins (%)						
Price reduction	15	20	25	30	35	40	
1%	7.1	5.3	4.2	3.5	2.9	2.6	
5%	50.0	33.3	25.0	20.0	16.7	14.3	
10%	200.0	100.0	67.7	50.0	40.0	33.3	
15%	—	300.0	150.0	100.0	75.0	60.0	

Price increases

As a corollary, look at the sales volume reductions which a price increase will support. It is more profitable to sell fewer items at a higher price.

	Percentage sales volume decrease supported by a price increase					
	Gross margins (%)					
Price increase	15	20	25	30	35	40
1%	6.3	4.8	3.9	3.2	2.8	2.4
5%	25.0	20.0	16.7	14.3	12.5	11.1
10%	40.0	33.3	28.6	25.0	22.2	20.0
15%	50.0	42.9	37.5	33.3	30.0	27.3

Marketing

The marketing of products or services is just as important for small businesses as it is for the giant fast-moving consumer goods companies such as Procter & Gamble.

Marketing is just as important for small businesses as for multinationals

Marketing means the consistent, coherent communication of benefits derived from the product or service to the consumer.

	Channels of communication	Customers
	Business name	
	Letterhead	
	Business card	
	Business stationery	DISTRIBUTORS
	Logo	
	Product names	
	Packaging	
	Delivery service	
	Vans	
	Overalls/tunics	
	Price-lists	
	Pricing	
	Discounts	RETAILERS
	Samples/prototypes	
	Editorial coverage	
	Personal selling, sales presentation, folders	
Benefits from the PRODUCT OR SERVICE	Telephone selling	
	Direct mail	
	Press/journal advertising	
	Radio/TV advertising	
	Poster advertising	END USERS
	Local media advertising/inserts	
	Product literature	
	Leaflets, brochures	
	Leaflet drops	
	Facility visits	
	Exhibitions, symposia, conferences	
	Promotions, competitions	
	After-sales/technical service	
	Complaints handling	
	Gifts	
	Giveaways (funny hats and tee shirts)	INFLUENCERS
	Posters	
	Yellow Pages and other directories	
	Clubs and societies	
	and the list goes on ... and on.	

Which channels will be cost effective for your business?

Promote benefits to the customer

You know what you make. Do you know what your customers buy?
Use this schedule to link the features you expensively build into your product or service to real benefits to your customers.

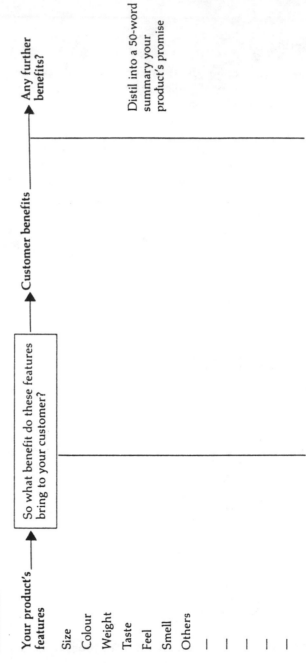

Your product's features

Size

Colour

Weight

Taste

Feel

Smell

Others

| | | | |

So what benefit do these features bring to your customer?

Customer benefits

Any further benefits?

Distil into a 50-word summary your product's promise

Selling, advertising and promotion should be based on the important customer benefits

Your target market

The target market is the group – or groups – of individuals to whom your business most successfully communicates its key messages in order for you to succeed.

What is your target market?

Define your target market by:

- Age
- Sex
- Location
- Social group
- Job title or occupation
- Special interests
- Life style
- Events/features
- Seasonality
- Other important descriptions

Estimate the number of individuals making up target group in your location:

Are there other target markets useful to your business which you can define?

Choosing your advertising medium

Selection of the best advertising medium is for the most part based on the costs of hitting the agreed target market. This table will allow media cost comparisons to be made.

NB. Origination, artwork and production costs must also be assessed. Where figures are difficult to obtain, some low-cost experimentation will be necessary. Monitoring of results is, of course, even more important than usual.

PRINT

	Audited circulation	Researched readership	Target market readership	Cost per 1000 target market	How does this medium relate to your product/service?
Newspapers					
Journals					

BROADCASTING

	Audience research	Target market audience	Cost per 1000 target market	How does this medium relate to your product/service?
Radio				
Television				
Cable television				
Cinema				

DIRECT SELLING

	List and delivery research	Target market delivery	Cost per 1000 target market	How does this medium relate to your product/service?
Direct mail				
Leafleting				
Telephone selling				

SHOWS AND EXHIBITIONS

	Attendance	Target market attendance	Cost per 1000 target market	How does this medium relate to your product/service?
Shows				
Exhibitions				
Conferences				

Monitoring of local advertising

Monitor direct response advertising to check its effectiveness

Direct response advertising (including coupons) lends itself to ready cost-effectiveness comparisons. This information should be collected for every campaign as a means of improving future campaigns.

This same table may be easily adapted to monitor direct mail and telephone sales campaigns.

Publication					
Frequency*					
Circulation (000s) (a)					
Number of insertions (b)					
Cost per insertion £ (c)					
Cost per 000 circulation £	$\frac{c}{a}$				
Cost of campaign £ (d) =	$b \times c$				
Number of enquiries (e)					
Number of quotations (f)					
Number of orders (g)					
Value of orders (h)					
Cost per enquiry £	$\frac{d}{e}$				
Cost per order £	$\frac{d}{g}$				
Cost per £ order value	$\frac{d}{h}$				

*Quarterly, monthly, weekly or daily

PRESS RELEASE

FREE ADVERTISING THROUGH EDITORIAL

Small businesses are full of news. News about people, products, premises, policies and progress. But surprisingly, the low cost promotional opportunities through news releases are neglected by small business.

To put this right, build a story round people and their success. Keep to the facts. Write the story in short sentences. Summarise the story in the first paragraph. Get the story typed with wide margins, double spaced. Include interesting quotations from key people. Avoid underlining and indiscriminate use of capital letters. Spell numbers one to nine, thereafter use figures. Use eight inch by five inch black and white photographs where possible. But photographs need clear accurate captions attached to them.

Select your target publications to include local, regional and national press, appropriate trade and technical publications, radio and television. Be sure to get your material to them by their copy date.

ENDS ...

Contact: Name   Phone

                    Address

                                 Date

Direct mail reduces marketing costs and gains new customers

Mr J Smith
Managing Director
Buggins Ltd
Industrial Estate
Newtown NW1 0WN

Dear Mr Smith

Would you like to reduce marketing costs? Would you like new customers?

For small but growing businesses like yours, DIRECT MAIL can be the most cost-effective way of bringing in new business.

Using bought-in mailing lists costing between £50 and £100 per thousand addresses, your message can be accurately delivered to your best prospects for between £200 and £300 per thousand. Using your own existing customer lists may be both cheaper and provide a better response.

These are the main questions for you to consider:

* What is the message to be communicated?
* What action do you want your prospect to take?
* What steps will you take to make it easy for your prospect to reply?
* What plans do you have to follow up non-responders?
* Have you the capacity and staff to handle the replies?
* What response rate are you expecting?
* Is the expense likely to produce a profit benefit?

> Experience in direct marketing by mail shows that mailings which arrive with your prospect on Tuesdays obtain the best response rates. Most successful direct marketers avoid holiday periods and 'silly seasons'.

CAPITALS, underlining, asterisks and postscripts all improve the chances of bringing in the business. Of course, keep it simple. Use short sentences. A personalised greeting, as in this letter, Mr Smith, and a legible signature, also help response rates.

Telephone your marketing adviser NOW to set up a small test campaign.

Yours sincerely

A. Seller

A. Seller

PS Did you know that the Post Office have free introductory offers on first mail shots and Business Reply licences? Get the facts from their Sales Office TODAY.

Methods of selling

Even the one-person company must sell hard. From the almost limitless list of sales opportunities, 25 of the most common are reviewed below.

How will you sell your product or service?

	To the trade	To the public	Comments	Estimate the cost
Personal visit	✓	✓	Gets in the way of other activities	
Salesperson	✓	?	Can be difficult to control	
Sales agent	✓	✓	Paid according to results	
Telephone sales	✓	✓	New skills	
Mailing	✓	✓	Low response rate. Can be targeted	
Poster		✓	Cheap to produce. Costly to post	
Radio	?	✓	Good for special segments of the market	
Television	?	✓	Expensive for small business. NB. Channel 4	
Newspapers	?	✓	Good cover. Wasted readership	

Journals
  Trade and technical
  General interest
  Special interest
	
	✓
	?
	
		?
		✓
		✓
			Response may be measurable	

Leaflets/brochures				
Mail order		✓	Diffucult to get into catalogue	

Shows/exhibitions
  Trade
  General
	
	✓
	
		✓
			Sometimes essential. Beware of unprofitable turnover	

Directories	✓	?	Yellow Pages and similar	
Party plan		✓	Beware of pyramid selling	

	To the trade	To the public	Comments	Estimate the cost
Multi-level marketing		✓	Gain personal experience	
Cinema	?	✓	Declining audiences. Good for some segments	
In-store demonstration		✓	Good visibility – check sales/profits	
Shop window cards	?	✓	Useful for trades/skills of local interest	
Sampling/trial use	✓	?	Expensive. May help an excellent product	
Editorial	✓	✓	Often overlooked – almost free	
Facility visits	✓	?	Visits to premises	
Complaints	✓	✓	Always a new sales opportunity	
Conferences	✓		Useful for specialised technical message	
Competitions/promotions	✓	✓	Can bring life to a dull product	

Exhibitions and shows

Exhibitions and trade shows can reveal new markets if your presence is well planned

Effective participation in a well-chosen exhibition can work wonders for a small, little known business seeking new business with individual, small, medium-sized and larger businesses. Common problems include:

- Choosing an unsuitable exhibition
- Underestimating the manpower and costs involved in the exhibition
- Forgetting to brief staff on the purpose of being there
- Omitting to follow up on all interested contacts after the exhibition.

Put simply, exhibitions are either horizontal or vertical.

Horizontal
Appealing to a wide cross-section of the population:

Business to Business Exhibition
Royal Show
Ideal Homes Exhibition.

Vertical
Appealing in depth to a specific audience:

Cruft's Dog Show
Congress of Cardiology
Offshore Inspection Repair and Maintenance Exhibition.

What local
      regional
           national
exhibitions meet your business needs?	

What are the costs involved?
   Space hire
   Stand design
      building
      services
      fitting
   Manning costs: people × cost/day
   Additional print material and gifts
   Travel, entertainment, accommodation
	£
	£
	£
	£
	£
	£
	£
	£

Total	£
+ Costs of not doing other priority things	£

What are your objectives?
   Direct sales off the stand
   Lead generation
   Product enquiries
   Product launch
How will follow-up be done?
	£
	Number:
	Number:

How many customers?

Answer: Fewer than you might first imagine

Customer calculations: how many do you need?

Estimated annual sales	£	(a)
Average size of sales transaction	£	(b)
∴ Annual number of sales transactions (a) ÷ (b)		(c)
Average annual frequency of customer purchase		(d)
∴ Annual number of customers* (c) ÷ (d)		(e)
Number of existing customers		(f)
Number of new customers needed (e) - (f)		

* For very small business, this number often lies in the range:
30 - for special trade selling operations
to
300 - for retail shops

BUT harder to obtain than you would ever have thought
Now look at the sales cascade (next page).

The sales cascade

In business start-ups and expansions, it is easy to overlook the workload encountered in generating new business. For example, for every five leads you have, you are only likely to make three relevant contacts. For every three contacts, only 1.5 get to first interview. If you work through the left-hand columns in the grid below, you will see that one order might need an original 101.25 contacts!

The number of interviews varies with the type of product or its market.

	Conversion rates from one level to the next		Number required to meet your sales plan	Time/cost involved £ or hours
	Typical	Your business		
Success One order		☐	Orders/customers required ☐	
Third interview Final bid for the business	3	☐	Third interviews ☐	
Second interview Handling objections Confirming details	1.5	☐	Second interviews ☐	
First interview The initial sales presentation	1.5	☐	First interviews ☐	
Contacts Conversation with named, relevant person, often prelude to an appointment	3	☐	Contacts ☐	
Leads An address, phone number, possibly a name. Can you generate enough?	5	☐	Leads ☐	
Multiplier effect	101.25			

Selling to large buyers

Large organisations like small suppliers

Most large organisations, such as ICI, Shell and local authorities, are keen to encourage the development of new small suppliers. But almost all of them need to be satisfied about the reliability and financial stability of the supplier.

The following form is reproduced from the Cheshire County Council procedure for becoming an approved supplier.

To: CONTROLLER OF SUPPLIES CHESHIRE COUNTY COUNCIL To be completed by the applicant	APPLICATION FOR INCLUSION ON THE COUNTY'S SELECT LIST OF CONTRACTORS
1. name of applicant (individual or organisation)	
2. address for normal business	
3. Sate whether independent, or whether subsidiary or member of group	
4. Turnover in £ sterling in respect of main goods (or services) being offered	
5. Percentage that above represents in relation to the overall turnover	
6. Specialities offered (goods or services)	
7. Extent of technical or other services available to your customers (as applicable). (a) technical (b) maintenance (c) design	(a) (b) (c)
8. Name other local authorities from whom you have been awarded contracts during the last five years (state full address)	

To: CONTROLLER OF SUPPLIES CHESHIRE COUNTY COUNCIL To be completed by the applicant	APPLICATION FOR INCLUSION ON THE COUNTY'S SELECT LIST OF CONTRACTORS
9. Other public organisations to whom you are currently supplying goods or services (state full addresses)	(a) (b) (c)
10. Value of such contracts	8(a) 8(b) 8(c) 9(a) 9(b) 9(c)
11. Any other relevant information which will aid the Controller of Supplies in the consideration of your application	

Sales control

To encourage attention to selling, this daily activity report has been drawn up. Even the one-person business can use the report, doing so for those days or part days in the week when active selling is done.

* Name/Town
** Sales call   C
   Sales interview   I
   Telephone interview   T
   Visit   V

*** Products by reference number
**** Miscellaneous, eg Order gained from
               Order lost to
***** Weekly and monthly figures may be carried forward

Daily activity report

Date

Customer*	Call type**		New (N) or existing (E) customer	Order size £	Products detailed***							Information****
	C or I	T or V			1	2	3	4	5	6	7	

***** TOTAL C =
TOTAL I =
TOTAL V =
TOTAL T =

TOTAL N =
TOTAL E =

SALES
£ _____
_____

MILEAGE

FINISH Miles –
START Miles –

TOTAL Miles – _____

EXPENSES – accommodation
– meals
– petrol etc

TOTAL £ _____

Control ratios such as:
  Orders/Interviews =
  Interviews/Calls =
  £ Order value/£ Travelling cost =
can be calculated.

Customer control

A customer record should exist for all major customers upon whom regular sales calls are to be made. A specimen is shown below.

Customer record

ACCOUNT   PHONE

CONTACT   Best Time/Day/Month

BUSINESS TYPE   POTENTIAL SALES
£   /year

Date	Payment status*	Objectives**	Results	Order value	Products	Objections***

* Checked prior evening
** Write objectives for next call to this customer immediately after sales call
*** For future interview planning

Channels of distribution

How will your goods reach the end user?   **Distribution**

What channels of distribution do your competitors use?

Use this map to identify the best channels for your products to reach the end user.

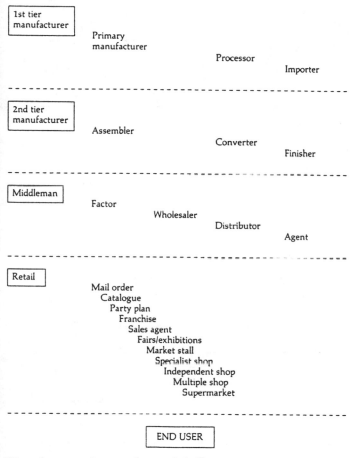

How do your chosen channels influence your:

* Prices?
* Discounts?
* Advertising?

Forecasting sales

Predicting your sales The firm which cannot generate a *sales forecast* has no reason to be in business. Nevertheless, sales forecasting is not easy, nor is it always accurate. Here are five ways in which your sales can be predicted. Use one or more methods.

1. Customers × orders

Average size of sales transaction	×	Customers		Sales £
£	×	/day /week /month /year	=	/day /week /month /year

Take seasonal factors into account.

2. Product/customer matrix

Customer	Z	Y	X	W	V	Product totals £
Product						
A						————
B						————
C						————
D						————
E						————
Customer totals £						Grand Total

NB. In many businesses 80 per cent of sales will come from 20 per cent of products/customers.

Have you asked your customers about their buying plans?

3. Extrapolation of present trends

	Actual				Forecast growth	
Annual sales	1993	1994	1995	1996	1997	1998
Divided by annual sales	÷	÷	÷	÷		
in previous year	1992	1993	1994	1995		
∴ Annual growth	%	%	%	%	%	%

4. 'Z' charts

The trend of moving annual total sales (= sales in last 12 months) will suggest future levels of sales. Intermediate sales targets can also be set. The example shows seasonal sales to December.

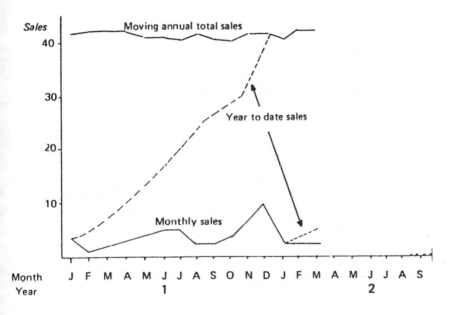

5. Market share

Year	Total market in units (a)	Competitors' market share %					Your company share % (b)	Your sales units (a) × (b)	Your selling price £/unit	Sales forecast £
		A	B	C	D	E				
1990 1991 1992										
1993 1994										

Now check:

	£	Units
Sales forecast		
Production capacity		

The marketing plan for bigger businesses

Compile a detailed marketing plan

For larger start-ups and major expansions, a written detailed marketing plan is desirable. Financiers may wish to see it incorporated into your business plan.

The marketing plan is the blueprint for marketing action and the document used for monitoring performance to show whether marketing objectives are being achieved. There are a number of possible formats in common use; this is one variation.

1. *Introduction and background*
   Assessment of market potential: market research information.
   Analysis of Strengths, Weaknesses, Opportunities, Trends (SWOT analysis).
   Analysis of competitive situation: existing market shares, competition, marketing strategies; possible counter moves, other likely reaction.
   Examination of human resources: key personnel, their responsibilities and potential.

2. *Marketing strategy outline*

Existing products: are they in growth, maturity, decline?

Proposed new products: pre-launch/launch planning, investment plans.

Written statements summarising product attributes: the brand propositions or brand intentions.

Features/Benefits analysis: key consumer benefits and competitive comparisons – Unique Selling Proposition (USP).

Proposed pricing strategy: what will the market stand?

Proposed distribution strategy: manufacturing/warehousing facilities, locations and costs.

3. *Strategic objectives. Where are we going?*

What targets, benchmarks of achievement do we set ourselves?

Are these detailed, specific and measurable?

Are they relevant, clearly understandable, challenging/demanding but achievable?

Marketing action plans to achieve above objectives, resources required and their deployment.

4. *Marketing monitoring and control*

Detailed breakdown of action plan (in 3 above) with monitoring methods.

| Sales projections Profit projections Market shares/penetration Selling expense | broken down by | Sales territory Product Key market Major accounts | – 1 year firm – 2 years indicative |

Sales operating budgets detailing each of the above features with projected attainment levels for each of the designated accounting/ trading periods (usually monthly, sometimes quarterly/weekly).

5. *Physical stock levels at key dates*

To meet seasonal variations permitting steady production with minimum inventory levels.

6. *Marketing support activities* needed to achieve the proposed objectives, for example:

   Sales training programmes
   Recruitment of additional personnel – job descriptions
   Advertising/sales promotion agency briefs
   Market research briefs etc.

7. *Longer-term strategic objectives*
   Research and development
   New product development
   New market development
   Diversifications etc.

For many projects, the marketing plan is an important component in an overall business plan.

◀ CHAPTER 5 ▶

NOW I NEED THE CASH...

Sources of finance

The sources of finance are basically few in number. The list is properly headed by: self, family and friends.

Where can you get the finance?

1. **Self, family and friends**
   Loans and equity
2. **Shareholders and directors**
   Loans and equity
3. **Internal company sources** (not applicable to start-ups)
   Retained profits, cash collection, stocks and creditors
4. **Clearing banks**
   Overdraft, short-, medium- and long-term loans
   Also some start-up and equity packages
   (Some building societies will provide long-term business
   development loans.)
5. **Second-tier finance**
   Hire purchase, leasing, contract hire, sale and leaseback, factoring
   and invoice discounting (see pages 75–6)
6. **Specialist financial institutions**
   Merchant banks and 3i
   Pension funds
   Investment trusts
   Insurance companies
   Plus: Banks other than clearing banks

Some local authorities, development corporations and enterprise boards

7. **Venture development capital**
   Venture capital funds
   Private investors

8. **Mergers and acquisitions**

9. **Grants**
   Government and local authority

10. **Money lenders**
    Mentioned for the sake of completeness only, and not to be used in business.

How much have 'Self, family and friends' provided? £

What proportion of total start-up funds does this come to? %

Second-tier finance

Additional finance – ask your accountant's advice

Brief descriptions of additional financing options are given below. Professional advice from your accountant should clarify which, if any, would suit the business best.

Hire purchase
- Outright ownership of the equipment at the end of the hire period.
- Capital allowances and other grants may be claimed at the outset by the hirer.
- Hire purchase usually requires a deposit, and hire payments comprise capital and interest – only the interest element is tax deductible.

Lease purchase
- Where no deposit is payable by the hirer, the agreement may be called lease purchase.

Leasing (sometimes referred to as tax or finance leases)
- Capital allowances and grants are held by the leasing company, and in some measure passed on as reduced rentals.
- At the end of the lease period, a secondary period of lease may be taken up as an option at a nominal rental. Alternatively, the

equipment may be purchased via a third party with drawback to the lessee.

- Lease rentals are treated as expenses, and therefore deductible against tax.
- Closed end leases run for a fixed term of one to five years. Open ended leases can be terminated at any time after the nominated minimum period. Balloon leases allow part of the capital payment to be made at the end of the lease agreement.

Contract hire (operating leases)

- Differs from finance leases in that the lessor is responsible for maintenance and, if necessary, replacement of the asset. Useful where the term of the lease is short when compared to the life of the assets.

Sale and leaseback

- An agreement between the seller and lessor wherein the seller undertakes to take a lease on the equipment, usually properties or large capital asset, for an agreed and long-term period. It releases cash for more profitable investment elsewhere but reduces the security in the business.
- An agreement between a firm and an institution wherein the firm sells its property, or a large item of equipment, to the institution, and at the same time takes out a long term lease on it for the institution.
- Releases capital for use in the business. Tax aspects need watching.

Summary

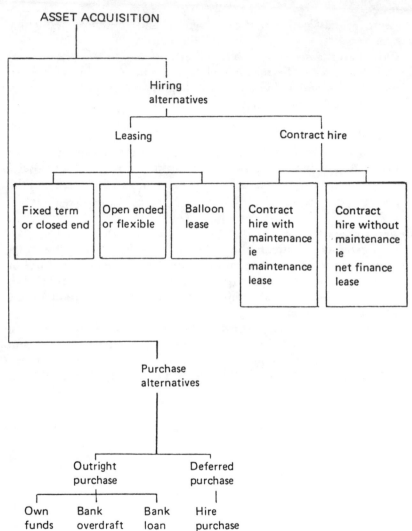

Factoring and invoice discounting

These two similar services may be used to bring a one-off improvement to cash flow.

Two services to improve your cash flow – at a cost

Factoring

Factoring is selling your business debts to the factoring company on a continuing basis in order to obtain immediate cash payments in place of the expected future payments. The factoring service includes sales ledger, invoicing, insurance, cash collection and credit control systems.

Advantages
Suits growth companies
Avoids extension of overdraft
Reduces administration
Reduces bad debts
Efficient paperwork

Disadvantages
Expensive – usually involves interest and service charges
More difficult for a young business to be accepted
Concern about effect on customers

Invoice discounting

A simple service which makes cash advances against some or all sales invoices.

Advantages
Cheaper than factoring
Customer relations unaffected
Suits growth companies
Avoids extension of overdraft

Disadvantages
Needs well-rated invoices
No help with sales administration
Expensive – usually involves interest and service charges
More difficult for a young business to be accepted by the finance house

The Association of British Factors and Discounters, 1 Northumberland Avenue, Trafalgar Square, London WC2N 5BW; telephone 0171 930 9112.

Further information

Equipment leasing

Leasing

For smaller businesses the place of leasing in the mix of financial opportunities is not always clear.

Advantages
Reduces capital need for start-up or expansion
Off balance sheet, therefore leaves balance sheet ratios unaffected
Quick, often easy, to arrange
Stable facility, cannot be withdrawn
'Full service' or flexible leasing options
Tax advantage to sole trader or partnership in first trading period
Useful when equipment with only limited life is needed, say three to five
    years, where capital could best be deployed for more long-term use

Disadvantages
Expensive
Restrictions on use of equipment and, for cars, a limit on tax relief
Medium-term inflexible contract
Asset now owned by user
Tax credits, if applicable, taken by lessor

**Points to watch
before entering a
leasing agreement**

Before completing a lease agreement:

1. Understand nature of proposed agreement.
2. Check term, interest rate, inclusions, exclusions.
3. Note any method of residual valuation and payment.
4. Note trade-in and cancellation penalties.
5. Obtain cash flow and after-tax costs.

Matching finance

**Never mix
long-term and
short-term financing**

Money raised by a business should be matched to the purposes to which it is to be applied.

A common error is to use an overdraft facility to purchase plant and equipment; never mix up long-term and short-term financing.

This list relates types, sources and purposes of finance.

Equity funding

Purpose of finance
Core finance
Permanent capital

Sources of equity funding
Self, family, shareholders and retained profits
Private investors
Development corporations and boards
Venture capital funds
Merchant banks
Insurance companies
Pension funds

Short-term funding (0–3 year money)

Purpose of finance
Short-term working capital needs
- seasonal requirements
- bridging finance

Sources of short-term funding
Self, family, directors' loans and retained profits
Debtors, stock reduction and extension of credit from suppliers
Clearing and other banks (overdraft)
Merchant banks
Finance houses
Leasing companies
Factoring and invoice discounting companies
Money lenders

Medium-term funding (2–10 year money)

Purpose of finance
Medium-term assets
- plant and machinery

Hard core working capital
- research and development

Sources of medium-term funding
Self, family, directors' loans and retained profits
Clearing and other banks (term loan and Loan Guarantee Scheme)
Development corporations and boards
Merchant banks
Finance houses
Leasing companies
Central and local government loans and grants
EC loans

Long-term funding (10–25 year money)

Purpose of finance
Long-term assets
- land, buildings

Corporate development

Sources of long-term finance
Self, family, directors' loans and retained profits
Clearing and other banks
Some building societies
Development corporations and boards
Merchant banks
Finance houses
Leasing companies
Central and local government loans and grants
EC loans
Insurance companies
Pension funds

Cash required to start the business

Forecast the cash you will need – don't underestimate your needs

The cash position is calculated in the forecasts for years 1 and 2 (see pages 82–6). Without this calculation, there may be a tendency to underestimate the cash necessary to start the business.

It will be difficult to raise more than half the cash required to start the business from external sources, such as the bank.

This diagram shows the way cash flows out of, and later, we hope, back into a business. Its purpose is to encourage the calculation of the total cash needed to cover the worst cash position – this often occurs some months after start-up. When this figure is known, own cash 'o' and external cash 'x' from, say, the bank, may then be calculated.

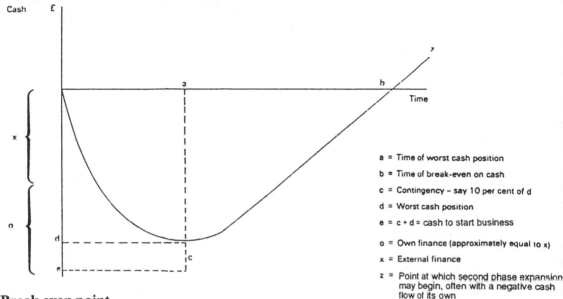

a = Time of worst cash position

b = Time of break-even on cash

c = Contingency – say 10 per cent of d

d = Worst cash position

e = c + d = cash to start business

o = Own finance (approximately equal to x)

x = External finance

z = Point at which second phase expansion may begin, often with a negative cash flow of its own

Break-even point

As part of the start-up – and as part of the business plan – it is instructive to calculate the sales revenue necessary to break even against total costs.

Calculate the break-even point: the sales you need to achieve to cover your costs

Sales revenue	–	Units × price
Variable costs	=	Those costs which vary directly with throughput, eg raw materials
Fixed costs	=	Those costs which remain unchanged by throughput, eg rent
Total costs	=	Variable costs + fixed costs

The break-even graph often looks like this:

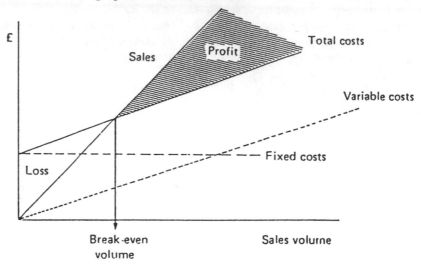

Now calculate:

$$\frac{\text{Break-even volume}}{\text{Production capacity}} \times 100 = \text{per cent}$$

$$\frac{\text{Break-even volume}}{\text{Current year sales target}} \times 100 = \text{per cent}$$

The higher these percentages, the less able the business is to withstand business uncertainty. Rethink when percentages exceed 70 per cent

$$\text{Gross margin \%} = \frac{\text{Sales revenue – variable cost}}{\text{Sales revenue}} \times 100$$

$$\text{Sales to break even} = \frac{\text{Fixed cost}}{\text{Gross margin}} \times 100$$

$$\text{Profit} = (\text{Sales revenue – sales to break even}) \times \frac{\text{Gross margin}}{100} \text{ (\%)}$$

Make sure your business plan includes the information listed here

The business plan

In an ideal world, the case presented to outside financial institutions should comprise the following. The proprietors also invest in the business; they too should have this information available.

1. *History of the business*

   A brief summary of the trading record and activities of the business since its inception, or during the last five years, whichever is the shorter. This paragraph would also include the numbers of employees through the period. List registered office, bankers, auditors/accountant, solicitor, and company registration numbers.

2. *Shareholders and senior managers*

   Include the major shareholders and their stakes. Describe the career details of the senior managers focusing on their successful track record throughout their careers.

3. *The market-place*

   Describe the market-place by, for example, geography, customers, business sector. Identify where possible total market potential, current existing market and your target share of market.

   Examine major competitors in the major markets identified, paying particular attention to their pricing and product improvement performance.

   Show the sales, marketing and distribution methods in use for the major parts of the business.

4. *Products and/or services*

   Describe the current range of products and services offered by the business, identifying the unique features and selling benefits associated with each one. Comment on the potential for *adding value* to existing products and services, and for developing totally new products and services.

5. *Business strategy (the five-year dream)*

   Write brief summary paragraphs that describe the overall business strategy, and the major functions of the business. These are likely to include capital structuring and financing, development, manufacturing, distribution, marketing, relationships with suppliers, premises, equipment. Note also the future management structure.

6. *Shorter-term objectives*

   A brief list of the major problems and opportunities that the management intend to face and to take up during the forthcoming 12 months.

   This paragraph should include the major assumptions made about conditions which will affect the business.

7. *Management information system*

   A short demonstration of how major functions of the business are positively controlled by the existing management. Examples include credit control, research and development, cost control, purchase control, production cost control, cash flow control, sales control.

8. *Financial requirements*

Tabular information designed to analyse the future financial requirements including the timing of intended expenditures, their sizes, the purpose of the expenditure and its planned benefit to the business.

For larger projects, break-even levels of sales and sensitivity analyses would be helpful. (Computer packages used by professional accountants can produce these simply and effectively.) Include the contributions to the future cash requirements to be made by the shareholders and other sources of capital. Describe the repayment plans.

9. *Basic financial information*

This should include the audited accounts for up to five years and the interim figures, ideally on a quarterly basis, for the current financial year. This should enable an up-to-date forecast for the current financial year to be made.

For future periods, information should be presented to cover the operating budget and hence the cash flows for the next 12 months analysed at least at quarterly, and preferably at monthly, intervals. Outline budgets and cash flows for the following two years would also be most helpful. Summarise this information in the profit and loss accounts and balance sheets.

10. *Security*

As a reserve document, not for immediate presentation, it is desirable to have available a summary of opportunities to provide personal security, business security, and the status of directors' loans.

Also have available the Memorandum and Articles of Association, and Partnership Agreements, where applicable. Prepare for a visit by the financier to the premises.

Business forecasts

Basic financial information must be collected

To help your accountant in the preparation of forecast cash flows, profit and loss accounts and balance sheets for the next three years, this basic data should be collected.

Business forecasts

VAT status

VAT rate	%
VAT pay date	

Financing

	Equipment (if applicable)		Deposit	
	Item	Cash cost £	Date payable	Size £
Loan • • •				
Hire purchase • • •				
Leasing • • •				

Operating statistics

		Year 1	Year 2	Year 3
Stock cover at year end				
raw materials	days			
work in progress	days			
finished goods	days			
Gross margin	%			

	Pre start-up or last financial year end
Receipts	
Proprietors'/shareholders' capital introduced	
Directors'/shareholders' loans	
Grants/other	

Payments

Fixtures/fittings
Equipment

Note. Enter description and *either* amount paid when bought outright, *or* complete financing

Registration	Not required/Voluntary/Compulsory*
Industry	Exempt/Zero rated/Mixed/Fully rated*
	* Delete as applicable

Advance		Repayments				Interest rate
Date	Size £	Date of first	Frequency	Size £	Term months	% APR

Current overdraft facility

£ _____

		Year 1	Year 2	Year 3
Average time to collect debts	days			
Average time to pay suppliers	days			
Materials/sales	%			
Direct labour/sales	%			
Cash sales/total sales	%			

Months												Year 1 Total	Quarters				Year 2 Total	Year 3 Total
1	2	3	4	5	6	7	8	9	10	11	12		1	2	3	4		

section above.

Now complete as much of this form as possible. With the exception of financing costs, write the figures on the basis of sales made and costs incurred (not as paid) and *exclusive of VAT*.

	Pre start up or last financial year end
Sales	

Direct materials
  Year end stock*
  Usage
  Purchases pattern	

NB. Total purchases for year = Closing stock + Usage – Opening stock. Purchases per period = Total purchases for the year spread according to purchase pattern.	
Direct labour (inc NI)	

Selling and distribution
  Carriage
  Packing
  Advertising and promotion
  Travel
  Sales salaries (inc NI)
  Sales commissions
  Others	

Occupation and administration
  Rent
  Rates
  Post
  Gas**
  Electricity**
  Water**
  Printing and stationery
  Insurances
  Repairs and maintenance
  Decoration and minor improvements
  Telephone***
  Professional fees
  Bank charges
  Salaries (inc NI)
  Others	

Financing costs (likely to be computed by your accountant)
  Overdraft interest
  Loan interest
  Hire purchase/leasing charges	

 * Pre start-up or last year end figures only
 ** Include connection charges
 *** Include connection, equipment, rentals and call costs.

Months												Year 1 Total	Quarters				Year 2 Total	Year 3 Total
1	2	3	4	5	6	7	8	9	10	11	12		1	2	3	4		

Basic rules of bank lending

How the banks operate

The clearing banks operate to simple lending rules. The business plan will recognise the rules and adapt to them.

1. **Equal contributions from the businessperson and the bank**
   - the '£ for £' rule, *or*
   - shareholders'/proprietors' equity: borrowing = 1:1

2. **Full security on the bank's lending**
   Often provided by:
   - personal guarantees
   - land (including buildings)
   - stocks and shares
   - life assurance policies
   - business assets, eg debtors, stock, fixed assets.

   The bank requires the security to be easy to value, readily marketable and easy to obtain good legal title to.

3. **Capacity to service interest charges**
   The degree to which planned profits exceed interest charges varies from bank to bank, but aim at a multiple of 4:1.

4. **Capability to repay the loan**
   The ability to repay within the term.

   The business plan will cover paragraphs 1 to 4 above and describe the nature of the proposition.

Finally, and probably most important:

5. **The borrower himself**
   - his integrity and reliability
   - his capability of carrying out his business plan.

Presenting your case personally to the bank

The bank manager is required to make an assessment of you and your project. While the business plan will say much about the project, the presentation interview will be the best time to communicate your enthusiasm, commitment and ability to manage. Use this ten-point checklist:

You and your business plan will be assessed by the bank. Check these points

1. Complete the business plan. Include details according to the size of the finance package required.

2. Identify a 'preferred' list of bank branches with named managers, your own bank to head the list.
3. Personalise the front page and the summary of the plan to each of the 'preferred' list bank managers.
4. Make an appointment of a sensible duration with a manager of appropriate seniority, having regard to the size of the financial package requested.
5. Leave the business plan with the manager three to four days ahead of the appointment.
6. Plan out the main points you wish to stress during your introductory comments at the interview.
7. Arrive early for the appointment, appropriately dressed.
8. Make main points simply and quickly, and in so doing show how well you understand the market for your product or service.
9. Answer the manager's questions to amplify and support the written business plan in a way which will demonstrate your personal capability to run the business and your commitment to it.
10. Ask for the finance specified on the front page (3 above).

The bank manager then has three responses:

	Responses	Your reaction
The bank manager's response	1. Agree	Ask about costs, interest rate and conditions, obtain facility letter.
	2. Want to think about it	Agree decision date, submit any further needed information.
	3. Reject	Find out objections and try to agree a re-presentation date.

The government-backed Loan Guarantee Scheme (LGS)

The LGS   Loans made under the LGS carry a premium of between 1.5 per cent to 2.5 per cent on the guaranteed element of the loan; but it can overcome some of the basic rules of bank lending (see page 86). Many restrictions are imposed on the uses to which the money may be applied. Contact your bank for details.

Benefiting from government grants

The DTI's grant aid programmes   Many grant aid programmes are available under the auspices of the Department of Trade and Industry.

While separate application forms tend to be applicable to each scheme, the following principles apply:

1. The company
(a) Must be viable (but not too viable)
(b) Must be well managed
(c) Should be likely to succeed
(d) Should contact Department of Trade and Industry. Try to get to know personally the officer responsible for the appraisal.

2. The project
(a) Must be viable
(b) Must have a clear end product
(c) Must be additional in that one of the following apply:
  - without aid the project would be cancelled
  - with aid, the project would be changed beneficially
  - its time-scale would be accelerated
  - it would be enlarged
(d) Should provide industrial and economic benefits
(e) Must be approved *before any expenditure* is incurred.

NB. The approval process itself can also take several months, so there is a need to plan ahead if advantage is to be taken of government grant aid.

Regional Development Grants are available in certain localities. Details should be obtained from the Department of Trade and Industry.

Business information document

The Prevention of Fraud Act places the entrepreneur at risk of heavy damages when the public is canvassed for money other than by licensed dealers in securities, eg banks and brokers. The activities and authorisation of investment businesses are now governed by the Financial Services Act 1986. When the time comes to seek additional investment in the business, summary information of the sort indicated below will determine the level of interest in the investor's side. An interested investor would subsequently expect a full business plan. It is important to seek professional advice before canvassing for finance. The rules are strict and must be observed.

Summary of information required when additional investment is sought

Main activities

Main markets and competition

Product range
- Existing products
- New products
- Patent position

Management team

Number of employees
- Past
- Present
- Projected

Main shareholders
(see table opposite.)

		Actual					Proposed	
Sales	£000	1992	1993	1994	1995	1996	1997	1998
Gross profit	£000							
Pre-tax profit	£000							
Balance sheet summary								
Issued capital								
Reserves								
Loans (with terms and security)								
Fixed assets								
Investments								
Current assets								
Current liabilities								
Cash requirements								
Capital expenditure								

◀ CHAPTER 6 ▶

...AND PREMISES

Working from home

Home may be a most suitable first base for the starter business. Whether it is legal and practical is a matter of fact and degree – this checklist may prevent expensive mistakes.

Checklist for working from home

Issue	Check with
Planning permission Building regulations	Planning Department Local authority
Restrictive covenants • Leasehold • Freehold	Lease agreement or title deed Solicitor
Mortgage	Building society, bank or mortgage company
Insurance	Insurance company
Tax consequences	Accountant
Other legislation relevant to your business plans	Local authority Solicitor
Disturbance	Neighbours
Effect on family life and social life	Family
Your own work efficiency at home	Self

If work at home is not practicable or excessive business use might lead to a liability for business rate, it may be worth contacting your local council about managed workshops or 'nursery' units. Such premises are specially designed for start-ups and young businesses.

Property requirements checklist

Search for the ideal business property

Before beginning the search, complete the 'Ideal\ column describing the property really needed to see the business through its early years. Fill in notes for interesting properties seen. Try to find at least three properties which come near to meeting the ideal needs

	Ideal	Property A	Property B	Property C

Type
  Warehouse
  Factory
  Office
  Shop

Location/Town

How Large? (in sq ft/metres)
  Warehouse
  Factory
  Office
  Shop

Access
  Pedestrian
  Vehicles
  Loading

Floor loading
Height
  Access doors
  Storage space
  Working space

Parking
  Essential
  Preferable
  Not important

	Ideal	Property A	Property B	Property C
Facilities				
Office accommodation				
Heating				
Lighting				
Ventilation				
Mains services				
– gas				
– electricity				
– water				
– drainage				
– finishes/insulation				
– security				
– lift				
When available				
Costs				
Purchase				
Rent – Length of lease				
Annual rent				
Rent review				
Premium				
Rateable value				
Legal (vendor's costs)				
Adaption and moving costs				
Constraints				
Fire hazards				
Planning permission				
Security				
Refurbishing				
Restrictive covenants				
Future expansion				
Neighbours				
Check also the following points:				
Noise				
Vibration				
Smells				
Overshadowing by buildings, trees etc.				

Rent reviews

Rents

Rent reviews have become a fundamental aspect of nearly every modern lease on commercial and industrial property. Landlords are reluctant to grant leases with the rent fixed for a long period, and tenants, notwithstanding their statutory protection, are reluctant to forgo their security by accepting short leases.

The complexities which normally prevail clearly require the experience and skills of professional advisers (see chart on page 95).

Lease renewals

Leases

In many cases, the expiration of a lease can have an effect similar to that of a rent review, in that the tenant may have been paying an historic rent, in which case the landlord will not have been receiving an economic return on his investment.

Upon the expiry of a lease the contractual commitment by both parties terminates, although the tenant usually has security of tenure under the provisions of the Landlord and Tenant Act 1954, supplemented by the Law of Property Act 1969; thus the relationship between the landlord and tenant will normally continue although the landlord may wish to exercise his statutory right to regain possession of the premises for the purpose of redevelopment of his own occupation, or one of the other statutory reasons.

The highly simplified chart on page 95 describes the process of renewals.

Whether one is landlord or tenant, it is essential to take professional advice at the earliest possible moment.

LANDLORD'S INSTRUCTIONS TO SURVEYOR

Landlord's surveyor serves notice to review the rent in accordance (where appropriate) with the terms of the lease, having carried out an inspection. Counter notice or objection must be served if required by lease. Time limits are strict. Legal advice is essential.

Tenant's instructions to surveyor and solicitor.

Surveyor liaises with tenant's solicitor then inspects the property. Investigation of lease terms. Measurement of premises. Collection and collation of comparable evidence. Surveyor's advice on rental value and lease terms.

Surveyor negotiates the rent with the other party.

If the tenant rejects proposed rent and there is an irreconcilable disagreement the lease will provide for an independent expert or arbitrator to be appointed.

Tenant accepts rent.

Appointment of an independent surveyor to act as an expert.

Appointment of arbitrator.

Expert invites written representations from each party's surveyor.

Arbitrator gives directions for conduct or arbitration either by written representation or hearing.

Hearing. Surveyor gives evidence in connection with valuation and is cross-examined thereon by counsel for other party.

Each party's surveyor prepares valuation with supporting evidence set out in *proof of evidence*.

If written submission — *points of reply* to other party's case are prepared.

New rental.

Tenant has to accept.

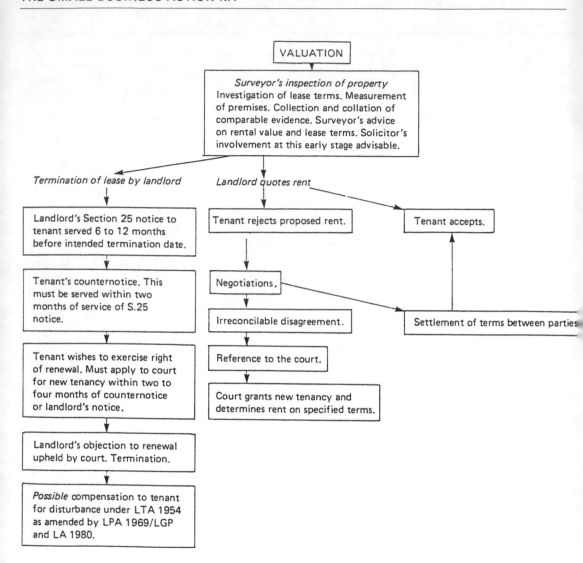

VALUATION

Surveyor's inspection of property
Investigation of lease terms. Measurement
of premises. Collection and collation of
comparable evidence. Surveyor's advice
on rental value and lease terms. Solicitor's
involvement at this early stage advisable.

Termination of lease by landlord

Landlord quotes rent

Landlord's Section 25 notice to
tenant served 6 to 12 months
before intended termination date.

Tenant rejects proposed rent.

Tenant accepts.

Tenant's counternotice. This
must be served within two
months of service of S.25
notice.

Negotiations.

Irreconcilable disagreement.

Settlement of terms between parties

Tenant wishes to exercise right
of renewal. Must apply to court
for new tenancy within two to
four months of counternotice
or landlord's notice.

Reference to the court.

Court grants new tenancy and
determines rent on specified terms.

Landlord's objection to renewal
upheld by court. Termination.

Possible compensation to tenant
for disturbance under LTA 1954
as amended by LPA 1969/LGP
and LA 1980.

The costs of getting into premises

Most attention is given to rent and rates.

Rent and rates

1st year costs

Rent: size		ft²	×	price	£ /ft²	£
Rates: poundage	£ /£		×	rateable value	£	£

TOTAL   £

But the total cost of getting into premises is *increased* by most of the factors listed below:

What premises cost

Other costs	Notes	Amount £
Advance rent	Often three months' rent	
Lease premium	Ask about reverse premium in a slack market	
Survey	Vital for full repairing lease	
Legal	Usually both landlord's and tenant's costs	
Insurances	See lease	
Property improvements	Some may be paid by landlord	
Property alterations	Permission required	
Planning permission	'Change of use' fees	
Services and service charges	3-phase electricity, gas, telephone, ventilation, caretaker, common areas. Who pays? How much?	
Security	Who provides? Who pays?	
Removal	Per quotation	
Disturbance to business	Usually underestimated	
Fire Environmental health and safety costs	} Check with relevant authorities	
May be aided by Moving-in package	Could include rent holiday, legal fees, improvements	

The routine of planning permission

Planning permission Professional advice will be necessary to help you unravel the intricacies of planning permission. This flowchart has been designed as a much simplified pattern of planning permission routine.

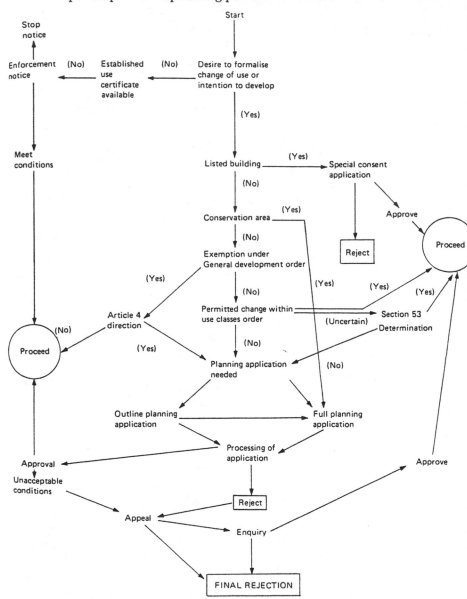

A guide to planning applications for commerce and industry

Applications, with appropriate fees, should be made to the Chief Planning Officer of your local council for permission to develop land. Applications are needed for new buildings and the change of use of existing buildings or other land.

Planning applications

The checklists below give a quick guide to the information which will generally be required, as a minimum, as part of the planning application. Basically there are two types of planning application, both of which are best prepared under professional guidance and should be discussed informally with an officer from the Planning Department *before* an application is made.

A. Outline application
An outline application can only be made for the erection of new buildings (or extensions to existing buildings). This will probably be appropriate in cases where it is initially necessary or advisable to establish the *principle* of new industrial development. This will be on land *not* in an industrial area or *not* allocated for industrial use in the local district plans.

An outline application needs:

1. Four completed application forms.
2. Four paper copies of a plan (preferably to a 1:2500 or 1:1250 scale) indicating the land in question within a red edge and any other land owned or controlled edged blue.
3. Any explanatory material which the applicant may wish to give, or which the local planning authority may require.

An outline permission granted will require the submission of a further application (a reserved matters application) giving full details of the new development.

B. Full (detailed) application
A detailed application needs:

1. Four completed application forms.
2. Four paper copies of plans showing:

(a) The area of land in question within a red edge.

(b) Plans and elevations of the proposed building(s), including details of materials and finishes.

(c) Details of the treatment of the remainder of the site, including size, location and surfacing of:

   (i) car parking areas

   (ii) loading, unloading and manoeuvring space

   (iii) open storage space (if any) and details of any proposed screening.

(d) Details of existing trees together with a proposed landscaping scheme.

Applications will also probably be required under the Building Regulations and an officer in the Planning Department will be pleased to provide advice on this aspect.

Local district or borough plans are available from the Chief Planning Officer, at the council offices.

Change of use: Is planning permission necessary?

Change of use

The Town and Country Planning (Use Classes) Order 1987 sets out use classes which cover the use of land and buildings. Changes of use which do not require planning permission are set out in Schedule 1 to the General Development Order 1977 as follows:

(a) From Class A3 (food and drink) or from a use for the sale or display for sale of motor vehicles to Class A1 (shops); and

(b) where the total floorspace does not exceed 235 square metres:

   (i) From B2 (general industrial) or B8 (storage and distribution) to Class B1 (business)

   (ii) From Class B1 (business) or B2 (general industrial) to B8 (storage and distribution).

The Use Classes Order defines a number of terms including 'shop', 'office', 'industrial building', 'light industrial building' and 'general industrial building'. The specified classes should not be stretched to include activities which do not clearly fall within them; unusual activities must be considered as separate uses in themselves. Changes of use to and from any such individual uses will generally require planning permission.

If you are in any doubt about the use class into which your activity falls, or whether planning permission is required for your use of a particular site or building, contact your local council Planning Department.

Categories of use classes

Class

1. Shop, except for sale of

    (i)   goods other than hot food
    (ii)   tickets or as a travel agency
    (iii)   sandwiches or other cold food for consumption off the premises
    or used:
    (iv)   as a post office
    (v)   for hairdressing
    (vi)   for the direction of funerals
    (vii)   for the display of goods for sale
    (viii)   for the hiring out of domestic or personal goods or articles
    (ix)   for the reception of goods to be washed, cleaned or repaired, where the sale, display or service is to visiting members of the public.

2. Use as an office for any purpose
3. Use as a light industrial building for any purpose
4. Use as a general industrial building for any purpose
5. (Special Industrial Group A). Alkali & Works Regulation Act 1096(a), which is not included in any of Classes 6, 7, 8 or 9
6. (Special Industrial Group B). Processes, carried on in or adjacent to a quarry or mine
7. (Special Industrial Group C). Processes based on the treatment of minerals except as an ancillary to the extraction itself
8. (Special Industrial Group D). Use for any of the following purposes:

    (i)   oils
    (ii)   cellulose
    (iii)   linseed oil
    (iv)   hot pitch or bitumen
    (v)   stoving
    (vi)   production containing organic chemicals

(vii)   rubber from scrap
(viii)   chlorphenols or chlorcresols
(ix)   acetylene
(x)   methyl, ethyl amine or acrylates

9. (Special Industrial Group E). Listed industries, businesses or trades
10. Wholesale warehouse or repository for any other purpose
11. Boarding or guest house, or an hotel
12. Residential boarding school, college or training centre
13. Public worship or religious instruction
14. Non-residential educational establishment
15. Health centre, school treatment centre, clinic, crèche, day nursery or dispensary, consulting room or surgery
16. Art gallery, museum, public library or reading room, public hall, exhibition hall
17. Theatre, cinema, music hall or concert hall
18. Dance hall, skating rink, swimming bath, Turkish or foam bath, gymnasium or sports hall.

◄ CHAPTER 7 ►

LEGAL AND TAX MATTERS

Legal format at start-up

The common view is that the 'sole trader' formula is preferable at lower levels of taxable profits. But there is no 'right' answer, and the decision ought to be made on the basis of what best meets the current and foreseeable business needs. Your solicitor or your accountant can help you to make the decision.

Ask your solicitor or adviser about the appropriate legal format for start-up

Sole trader

Advantages
No legal formalities
Total responsibility
Short-term tax benefits
Taxed as individual
Financial flexibility
May start at any time
Ease of winding up
Self-employed pension facility

Disadvantages
You stand to lose your personal assets if you go bust
No corporate pension provision
Loss of some social security benefits
Limited access to finance

Partnership

As for sole trader plus:

Advantages

Simple tax assessment

Disadvantages

Partnership agreement advisable

Difficult to grow through gaining new partners

Each partner responsible for all debts

Limited companies

Advantages

Limited liability*

Lower tax burden in many situations

Company tax burden at higher profit levels

Company pension schemes

Status/Image

May be easier to sell shares depending on initial structure

Loans and shareholders easily added to corporate structure

Employee status for social security benefits

* May be negated in practice by guarantees

Disadvantages

More costly to run

Trading allowed only after incorporation

Loss of profit sharing flexibility

Formal company meetings

Filing of accounts

Higher professional fees

Restricted loans to directors

Schedule E taxation for directors

All employees on PAYE

Corporation Tax liability

Partnerships

Unfortunately, a number of business partnerships have difficulties owing to the *absence* of a formal partnership agreement.

Partnership agreements should cover many considerations

A partnership agreement drawn up with your accountant's and your solicitor's help before the business begins should consider:

1. Members of the partnership
2. Period of the partnership: commencement, duration and termination
3. Name of the partnership
4. Business activities and location
5. Partnership premises including tenancy agreement/leases
6. Capital: sharing and interest thereon
7. Goodwill
8. Profit (and loss) sharing formula
9. Drawings on account of share of profits
10. Treatment of remuneration, eg partners' fees and legacies from clients of the firm
11. Books of account
12. Annual accounts including accounting date
13. Clients' monies, if applicable
14. Accountants
15. Bankers
16. Responsibilities of partners including holiday entitlement
17. Negative covenants
18. Motor cars
19. Outgoing partners' arrangements
20. Compulsory retirement at given age
21. Admission of new partners
22. Pensions, annuities and insurance arrangements
23. Tax provisions and continuation election
24. Covenants in restraint of trade
25. Dissolution of partnership
26. Expulsion of partners
27. Serving of notices
28. Partnership meetings and voting thereat
29. Arbitration.

Business names

Naming the business

The name a business uses can be a great help to the business but there are a few constraints on the freedom of choice.

Sole trader

1. The individual's own name brings no extra requirements, eg Smith, J Smith.
2. A different name requires:

   - Letterheads, orders, invoices, receipts, payment demands to bear name and address of owner
   - A notice of the name and address to be prominently display in all business premises
   - An answer, in writing, to any request for owner's name and address.

Partnership

As above, except for partnerships of more than 20 persons for which additional regulations apply.

Limited companies

Subject of the approval of the Registrar of Companies, with requirements to avoid:

   - The same name as another company
   - Criminal, offensive or misleading names
   - Names used by certain qualifying entities (eg bank)
   - Names connected with the government or royalty, or implying national or international pre-eminence.

There is also a statutory list of words for the use of which prior approval must be obtained.

Formation of limited companies

Forming a limited company

For some people it may be desirable to form a limited company at the time of start-up. For others, successful expansion may prompt professional advisers to suggest incorporation (formation of a limited company).

1. Memorandum of Association sets out:
(a) Company name
(b) Whether the registered office is in England, Wales, Scotland or Northern Ireland
(c) The company's objectives
(d) A statement of the shareholders' liability
(e) The number of authorised shares by type.

2. Articles of Association typically set out:
(a) The procedure for calling general and extraordinary meetings
(b) The responsibilities and rights of directors
(c) Procedure for election of directors
(d) The company's borrowing policies
(e) Control of shares

A set of model Articles is usually available from accountants and solicitors incorporating the various provisions required by the Companies Acts.

3. Declaration of Compliance with the Companies Acts.
Your solicitor and your accountant will help you to complete the following documents:

Accounting reference date
Share allotment
Statement of first directors and secretary and intended situation of registered office
Statement of change of directors or secretaries
Notification of change of registered office.

Following the submission of these documents by your accountant or your solicitor to the Registrar of Companies, and his acceptance, the Certificate of Incorporation will be issued. The Certificate and registration date should be displayed on public view, while the registration number and other formal details must appear on official company stationery.

Responsibilities of company directors

Many people see the position of being a company director as a status symbol. The responsibilities of being a company director, some of which

The responsibilities of being a director

107

are given below, should encourage you to discuss your individual case with your solicitor or your accountant.

- Directors have to attend board meetings.
- They have to disclose their private interests and shares in the company.
- Directors must act with diligence and honesty, and know what is going on.
- They are liable for all debts of the company if, knowing it is insolvent, they allow the company to trade into further debt.

Furthermore, there are these constraints on company directors:

- By the Articles of Association, directors are granted powers which may not be exceeded.
- They are elected and may be removed.
- They are subject to special requirements by the Inland Revenue with regard to expenses and perquisites.
- Normally, directors may not borrow money from the company in excess of a certain threshold (increased periodically by the Chancellor of the Exchequer).

Value added tax (VAT)

VAT

VAT collected by HM Customs & Excise. Most businesses have to learn to live with it.

1. Reasons for registering
   Compulsory when turnover reaches or is likely to reach the VAT threshold.
   High input VAT paid, which is recoverable.
   Credibility with other traders.
   NB. VAT registered customers can claim back invoiced VAT.

2. Method of registering
   Discuss with your accountant first.
   Telephone VAT office and ask for literature, including any special leaflets relating to your industry.

3. Operating the scheme
   Maintain up-to-date, accurate books – see your accountant.

Prepare to be inspected by an officer of HM Customs & Excise.
Include VAT payments/receipts in cash flow projections.
Keep all invoices as evidence of VAT payments.

VAT is compulsory when turnover from zero-rated and standard rated goods and services exceeds or is likely to exceed the currently prescribed annual limit. The calculation is based on the past 12 months' turnover and the small business must review turnover monthly and register for VAT if at the end of any month the value of taxable supplies in the last 12 months exceeds the limit, or there are reasonable grounds to believe it will exceed the limit in the next 30 days. Registration takes effect from the end of the month in which the 30 days fall, or such earlier date as may be mutually agreed.

HM Customs & Excise are usually most helpful when queries and uncertainties are put to them. Also, there is a free helpline for people with queries regarding basic VAT registration. Call: 0345 143 143.

Tax and the newly self-employed

Discuss your tax with your accountant

A few years ago, the chancellor of the day announced a simpler basis for taxing businesses, so that new businesses starting after 5 April 1994 will be taxed on the actual profits for each tax year. This is called the current year basis. Businesses started before 5 April 1994 have moved on to these new tax rules following the 1996/97 transitional rules.

New self-assessment rules also came into being in 1996/7, so your accountant will have to prepare your accounts promptly. Automatic penalties loom for those who fail to return their SA forms by the due date.

As an *employee*, your income tax and National Insurance contributions were deducted from your renumeration before you received it: that is, you could spend what you received. Now that you are self-employed, your annual income tax and Class 4 National Insurance contributions will normally be payable in two halves: the first half on 31 January in the tax year, and the second half six months later, on 31 July.

Check what your liabilities are and when you have to pay them

Furthermore, your income tax and Class 4 National Insurance bills for the first two or even three tax years are likely to land in your lap together when you least expect them, with only a few days before payment has to be made. You must therefore find out from your accountant what your liabilities are likely to be, and when you might have to pay them.

- It is essential that your cash forecast takes account of your income tax and National Insurance payments so that the cash is there when needed.

Licences and permissions

Licences and permissions

A wide variety of laws and regulations control and limit certain types of businesses. An indication of licences in which you could be involved follows:

Legislation	*Covering*	
Consumer Credit Act 1974	Credit sales Dealing in securites	
Transport Act 1983	Operators' licences	
Medicines Act 1968	Human and veterinary medicines	
Solicitors' Act 1974		
Veterinary Surgeons Act 1966 and similar Acts	Practice in certain professions	Professional advice from your solicitor is recommended
Registered Homes Act 1984	Nursing homes	
Betting, Gaming and Lotteries Act 1963	Gambling and gaming	
Employment Agencies Act 1973	Employment agencies	
Children's Act 1975	Employment of child	
Town & Country Planning Acts 1963–84	Planning permission	

The local Borough or District Council handles planning permission, and a range of other licences such as:

Music and dancing
Late night refreshments

Cinema
Theatre employers
Theatre performance of plays
Pleasure boats
Lotteries and amusements
Amusements with prizes
Food and ice cream
Hawkers
Street and house-to-house collections
Petroleum and paint storage
Private hire vehicle operator
Private hire and hackney carriage driver's licence
Private hire and hackney carriage vehicle licence
Pet shop
Breeding of dogs
Boarding of dogs
Riding establishments
Slaughterman
Dealing in game
Scrap metal dealing
Explosives and fireworks
Shops and factories

Make first contact with the Planning Department or Environmental Health Department.

For public houses, licensed restaurants, hotels, boarding houses and wine bars, contact the Justices' Clerk.

Data protection

The Data Protection Act 1985 requires any business that keeps records of personal data on individuals in computer files to register with the government. Existing data files should be registered. New computerised records need immediate registration. Further information is available from the Office of the Data Protection Registrar, Springfield House, Water Lane, Wilmslow, Cheshire SK9 5AX; telephone 01625 535711.

Data protection

Business insurance

Insurance

In addition to the insurance that an individual will take out in his or her private life, the business owner should consider seriously the insurance he or she will need at business start-up, and then throughout a business career. The following list will help you to decide which to take out, and when.

	Immediate cover (date)	To be covered by (date)	Not relevant in foreseeable future
1. Fire and special perils			
2. Advance and consequential loss following fire, special perils, sprinkler damage and machinery breakdown			
3. Burglary			
4. Employer's liability			
5. Professional indemnity			
6. Directors' and officers' liability			
7. Public and product liability			
8. Money			
9. Commercial vehicles			
10. Goods in transit			
11. Private cars			
12. Mobile plant			
13. Contractors all risks			
14. Engineering – lighting equipment, electrical plant boilers, and general equipment			
15. Plate glass			
16. Key person (including personal accident and sickness, private hospital costs), group personnel			
17. Life assurance and pensions			
18. Computer and computer records			
19. Legal costs and expenses			
20. Livestock			
21. Marine and aircraft insurance			
22. Political risk			
23. Credit insurance			
24. Fidelity			

Which of these covers are you *required by law* to take out?

Obtaining UK registered design protection

Design protection

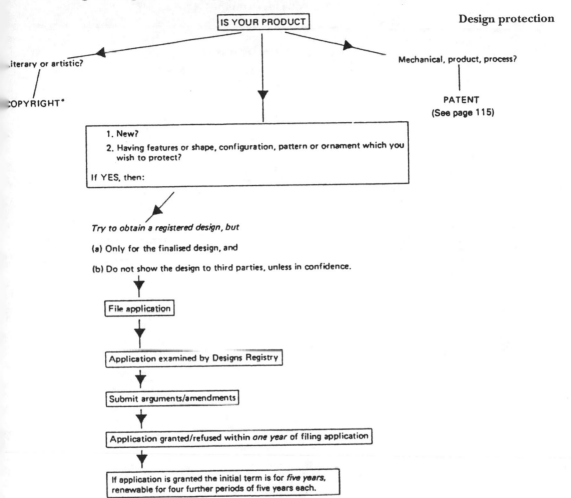

IS YOUR PRODUCT

Literary or artistic?

COPYRIGHT*

Mechanical, product, process?

PATENT
(See page 115)

1. New?

2. Having features or shape, configuration, pattern or ornament which you wish to protect?

If YES, then:

Try to obtain a registered design, but

(a) Only for the finalised design, and

(b) Do not show the design to third parties, unless in confidence.

File application

Application examined by Designs Registry

Submit arguments/amendments

Application granted/refused within *one year* of filing application

If application is granted the initial term is for *five years*, renewable for four further periods of five years each.

* In many cases products of an orginal design are protected from illicit copying by the Copyright, Designs and Patents Act. This protection is inherent and immediate.

Professional advice at an early stage will help you to assess the value and chances of obtaining design registration. Please see also the free official information pack, available from the Patent Office, Information and Marketing Services, Cardiff Road, Newport, Gwent NP9 1RH; 01633 814000.

Obtaining a UK patent

UK patents

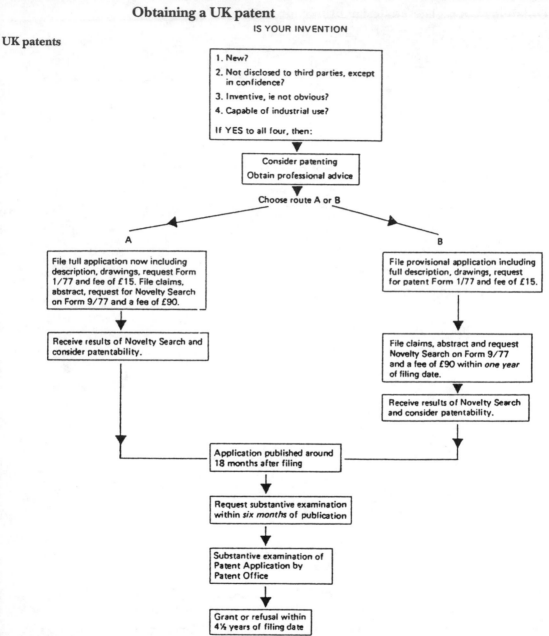

IS YOUR INVENTION

1. New?
2. Not disclosed to third parties, except in confidence?
3. Inventive, ie not obvious?
4. Capable of industrial use?

If YES to all four, then:

Consider patenting
Obtain professional advice

Choose route A or B

A

File full application now including description, drawings, request Form 1/77 and fee of £15. File claims, abstract, request for Novelty Search on Form 9/77 and a fee of £90.

Receive results of Novelty Search and consider patentability.

B

File provisional application including full description, drawings, request for patent Form 1/77 and fee of £15.

File claims, abstract and request Novelty Search on Form 9/77 and a fee of £90 within *one year* of filing date.

Receive results of Novelty Search and consider patentability.

Application published around 18 months after filing

Request substantive examination within *six months* of publication

Substantive examination of Patent Application by Patent Office

Grant or refusal within 4½ years of filing date

Because of the complex nature of the above, you should take professional advice.

Obtaining UK trade mark registration

A trade mark is a word, device, etc, which is used to identify a trader's goods and to distinguish such goods from others. If the trade mark is sufficiently distinctive, statutory rights in it may be obtained through registration.

Trade mark registration

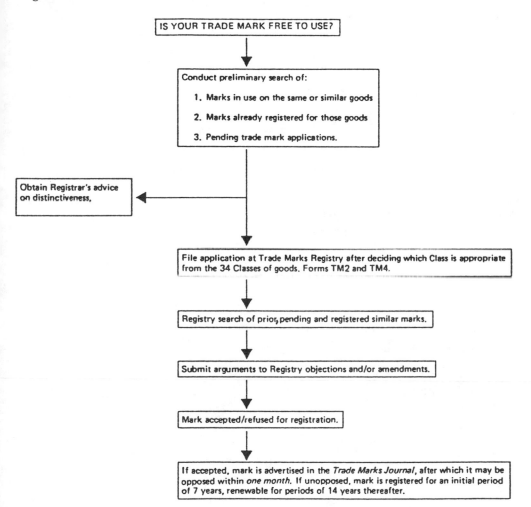

IS YOUR TRADE MARK FREE TO USE?

Conduct preliminary search of:

1. Marks in use on the same or similar goods

2. Marks already registered for those goods

3. Pending trade mark applications.

Obtain Registrar's advice on distinctiveness,

File application at Trade Marks Registry after deciding which Class is appropriate from the 34 Classes of goods. Forms TM2 and TM4.

Registry search of prior, pending and registered similar marks.

Submit arguments to Registry objections and/or amendments.

Mark accepted/refused for registration.

If accepted, mark is advertised in the *Trade Marks Journal*, after which it may be opposed within *one month*. If unopposed, mark is registered for an initial period of 7 years, renewable for periods of 14 years thereafter.

Professional advice is strongly recommended in all matters relating to trade marks in view of the possibility of confusion and/or passing off occurring, with resultant litigation.

CHAPTER 8

BEGINNING TO MANAGE

Documentation for start-up

**Order your
business stationery**

Paperwork should be kept to a minimum. Nevertheless, paper records are required to protect you and your business. Most of these items will be required before start-up:

	Dates		
	Designed	**Ordered**	**Delivered**
Letterhead			
Business card			
Publicity material			
Price-lists			
Order pad			
Invoice/delivery/credit note set			
Monthly statement			
Petty cash voucher book			
Cheque book			
Bank paying-in book			

The letterhead and business card may well be the first contact a customer has with your business.

Will they say about you what you want them to say?
In the case of a private limited company, the letterhead must show the address of the registered office, the registration number, the word *Limited* or *Ltd*, all or none of the directors, and the VAT number if registered.

Basic business records

No business can be properly run without adequate records. This short list covers the *absolute minimum* of information. Records should be written up daily or weekly, and be completely backed up by receipts, vouchers etc.

Business records must be kept up to date

1. *Cash book*
    (a)   Record cash sales and payments made from cash transactions.
    (b)   Record payments in and out of bank.
    (c)   Show VAT on payments as applicable.
2. *VAT records* (if applicable)
    (a)   Show how VAT return figures have been calculated.
    (b)   In addition, non-retailers must maintain a list of sales invoices issued.
3. *Petty cash book* (where applicable)
    Small cash expenses should be kept on an imprest basis and should show VAT where applicable.
4. *Wages book, wage slips*
    Summary information to meet the needs of the employee and the Inland Revenue.
5. *Order and delivery books*
    Purchase and sales, orders and deliveries.
6. *Overdue accounts book*
    Debtors and age analysis of debts for all credit sales.

Professional advice from your accountant should establish the most appropriate records for the business. If you follow this advice, it will tend to reduce his or her fees.

Some businesses may find the services provided by a contract bookkeeping service cost-effective.

The bank account

Think about bank accounts well before start-up

Few businesses can operate outside the banking system. These details should be covered well before start-up date.

1. *How many accounts?*

	Needed (tick)	Date arranged	Note
Business current account			Overdraft facility
Business deposit account			Interest rate?
Business loan accounts			
Personal current account			
Personal deposit account			
Personal loan account			
Personal 'tax' account			To cover future tax demands

Don't have more accounts than you need and can manage.

2. *Bank statements*
   Frequency (delete as applicable)
   Daily
   Weekly
   Monthly
   Quarterly

   The bank reconciliation (see below) should be made for each statement.

3. *Signatories*
   Obtain bank mandate form.
   Use crossed cheques.
   Name two signatories whenever practicable.

   NB. Two signatories may lead the Inland Revenue to argue that a 'sole trader' is now a 'partnership'. Complete cheque book stubs fully and accurately.

4. *Charges*

It all costs money. Discuss with your bank manager what you can sensibly do to minimise bank charges. Get quotations from other banks.

Bank reconciliations

A bank statement is produced by the bank at your request. A weekly statement would be right for many businesses.

Reconcile your bank statement and the bank report

A bank position or report shows your own latest figures of your bank account.

The *bank statement* and the *bank position or report* should be reconciled from time to time – often weekly. This format shows how to do the reconciliation.

1. Balance according to bank statement £

2. Add monies paid in but not cleared by the bank
   (deduct if bank statement shows an overdraft) £

3. Deduct cheques drawn but not entered by the
   bank (add if bank statement shows an overdraft) £ _____

4. Balance according to books £ _____

                        Difference, if any £ _____

Any difference should be investigated immediately.

NB. Interest on any overdraft, and bank charges, will be debited to the account automatically, usually every quarter.

Purchasing practice

Good purchasing is a vital element in all businesses but especially in retailing and manufacturing. This checklist has been designed as a guide to purchasing.

A checklist guide to good purchasing practice

119

Action	Check
1. Analyse goods to be purchased	Specification complete, up to date and accurate
2. Identify vendors who can supply	Provision for quality assurance Competitiveness Financial status
3. Issue enquiries	Instructions clear Terms of purchase specified Delivery requirements Any additional requirements
4. Receive quotations	Equipment described meets specification Analyse vendor's 'Conditions of Sale' and compare with your 'Conditions of Purchase' Price variation or fixed price? Payment terms and quantity discounts/rebates Validity Warranty Delivery period
5. Evalue quotations	Comparisons 'like for like' Total cost of order in consideration of any advance payments Current workload/financial status Delivery period
6. Choose best option	After considering 4 and 5 above
7. Place order	Terms of order are agreeable to vendor and purchaser Any additional requirements
8. Expedite acknowledgement	Check 'Terms of Acknowledgement' are in agreement with 'Terms of Order'
9. Monitor progress of order	Inspection/expeditor reports as necessary
10. Approve invoice payment	Check goods received in good order Verify any extras/reductions Obtain Certificates of Ownership if appropriate.

The routine of business accounting

Effective financial control is essential for business success

There is no substitute for keeping up-to-date financial control. Check that you meet these suggestions:

	Daily	Weekly	Monthly	Quarterly	Six-monthly
Check cash takings against till roll (retail)	✓				
Note cash position	✓				
Write up day books	✓				
Raise invoices	✓				
Bank cash/cheques	✓				
Check deliveries against delivery notes	✓				
Pay wages		✓	or ✓		
Draw cheques		✓			
Prepare weekly summaries		✓			
Do bank reconciliation		✓	or ✓		
Follow up overdues		✓	✓		
Issue statements			✓		
Total and summarise ledgers			✓		
Authorise salaries, tax and NI			✓		
Compare actual with budgeted sales and expenses			✓		
Update cash flow projections			✓	or ✓	
Take raw material, work in progress and finished goods stocks			✓	or ✓	
Prepare age analysis of debtors and creditors		✓	or ✓		
Pay VAT				✓	
Prepare trading account			✓	or ✓	or ✓
Prepare interim accounts			✓	or ✓	or ✓
Complete tax planning				✓	or ✓
Do sales and expenses budget updates				✓	

Precisely who is responsible for each item of work?

How do you know it is being done properly and on time?

Annual accounts

Annual accounts – a legal requirement for companies

Annual accounts should be completed within a few weeks of the financial year end, and include:

1. Profit and loss account
2. Balance sheet
3. Sources and application of funds (companies)
4. Notes and analyses
5. Directors' Reports (companies)

Annual accounts are a legal requirement for companies. Sole traders and partnerships need them for the taxman, and probably the bank. Usually they are prepared by your accountant.

Annual accounts provide insufficient information for the running of most businesses. To keep control of a business you must have constant up-to-date information, which should be discussed with your accountant.

Tick your plan

How often do you want to have:	Monthly	Quarterly	Six-monthly
Trading accounts	☐	☐	☐
Profit and loss accounts	☐	☐	☐
Balance sheets	☐	☐	☐
Sources and application of funds statements	☐	☐	☐
Working capital movements	☐	☐	☐
Summarised cash movements	☐	☐	☐

Tick your plan

	Monthly	Quarterly	Six-monthly
Cash flow projections	☐	☐	☐
Discussion of current trends and prospects	☐	☐	☐
Review of overall plans	☐	☐	☐

NB. Some of the above are alternatives depending on the amount of information considered necessary for effective control.

Marginal product costing

As a prelude to any sales, the businessperson should calculate his or her cost build-up using a format similar to this.

Marginal product costing

Direct material costs

	Cost	×	Usage*	=	Materials cost
Materials	£ per unit	×	Units per product, job etc	=	£ per product, job etc
(i)					
(ii)					
(iii)					
(iv)					
(v)					
(vi)					
(vii)					
	Total Direct material cost (A)	=		£	

* Including wastage/losses

Direct labour costs

	Cost**	×	Usage	=	Labour cost
Operations	£ per unit	×	Standard hours per product, job etc	=	£ per product, job etc
(i)					
(ii)					
(iii)					
(iv)					
		Total Direct labour cost (B)		=	£

** Full cost, not wage rate

Overhead costs

For example: *Annual Cost £*
Marketing costs
Travel
Rent, rates
Insurance
Post, telephone
Heating, lighting
Repairs, maintenance
Administration salaries, NI
Professional fees
Loan and overdraft interest
Depreciation
Others

                                          Total cost   _____   (D

	Products				
	1	2	3 etc		
Selling price (£)					(E)
Product, jobs etc (number)					(F)
Total sales (£)					(G = E × F)
Total direct materials (£)					(H = A × F)
Total direct labour (£)					(I = B × F)
Total variable cost (£)					(J = H + I)
Contribution to overheads and profit (£)					(K = G – J)

Overhead cost (£)   (D)

Profit (£)   (K – D)

$$\text{Gross margin } \% = \frac{\text{Contribution} \times 100}{\text{£ Sales}} \qquad (\frac{K}{G} \times 100)$$

These figures may help with:

- New price structures
- Changes to product mix
- Adjustments to size of labour force
- Make or buy-in decisions
- Capital expenditure to save labour costs

Margins and mark-ups

Business people involved with retailers need to be familiar with these two expressions.

Margins and mark-ups

$$\text{Margin} \quad = \frac{\text{Selling price} - \text{buying price}}{\text{Selling price}} \times 100 = \qquad \%$$

$$\text{Mark-up} \quad = \frac{\text{Selling price} - \text{buying price}}{\text{Buying price}} \times 100 = \qquad \%$$

Try these calculations:

Selling price (excl VAT)	Buying price (excl VAT)	Percentage margin	Percentage mark-up
£1.00	50p		
£1.50	£1.00		
£2.66	£2.00		
£3.00	£2.40		
£4.00	£3.60		

Cash collection

Collecting the cash that is owed to you

A sale is not a sale until it is paid for (although it will go into your accounts as soon as it is invoiced)!

Wherever credit is given, cash flow can *always* be improved. Improve cash collection by:

1. Having a named person responsible for cash collection.
2. Setting cash collection targets and measuring performance.
3. Taking out credit references and setting credit limits.
4. Specifying payment date on:

   - quotation/estimate
   - price-list
   - delivery note (file signed copy)
   - invoice statement

   And mentioning it in all relevant conversations.

5. Issuing invoice immediately and accurately on completion/delivery of work. Cross reference to order numbers. Deliver to correct address as specified by the buyer.
6. Establishing date of automatic follow-up by:

   - statement
   - letter of demand
   - telephone   } Don't be taken in by excuses!
   - stop supply
   - letter of legal action

7. Considering prompt payment discounts, deposits, prepayments and stage payments.
8. Proceedings through:
   County Court (limits vary according to type of case).
     Small claims procedure (limit £1000)
   High Court.

9. Pressing for execution of any court order.
10. Ceasing to supply slow payers on credit: use proforma invoice.
11. Considering non-recourse factoring and bad debt insurance.

Is credit given measured?

Days

1. $\dfrac{\text{Total outstandings} \times 365}{\text{Annual sales}}$ = ☐

2. Total outstandings offset against immediate past invoices = ☐

3. What were comparable figures:
   last year? ☐
   in previous year? ☐

4. What do competitors give? ☐

The integrated computer accounting package

To the question 'Should I buy an integrated computer accounting system?' there is no immediate answer.

Take advice about buying a computer accounting package

Take expert advice, and remember that *rarely will the computer bring cost reductions*, but it may enable more work to be handled.

Interrelations in the integrated package

In a fully integrated computer accounting package, the full range of accounting functions – sales, purchases, accounting, P&L accounts, trial balances, stock control and the rest – can be handled. The following diagram, shows the way in which these functions interrelate.

The full range of accounting functions can be handled

127

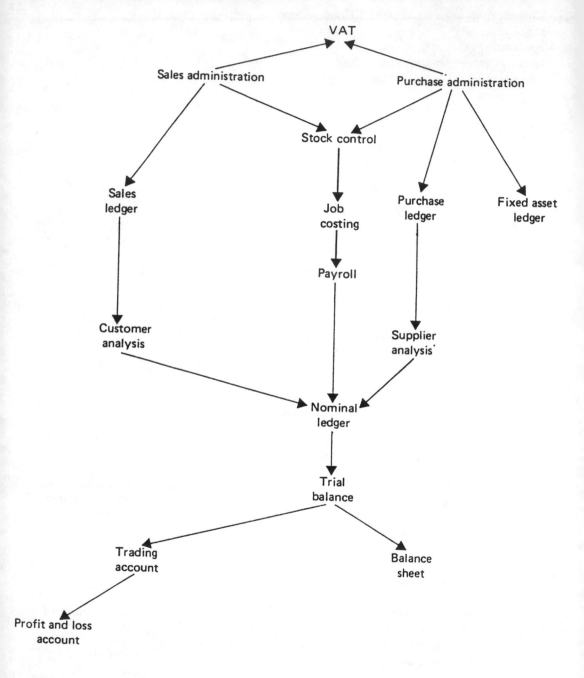

Credit cards

From the point of view of a merchant or trader, the use of a credit card can be a considerable advantage.

Advantages of the credit card

1. The merchant obtains immediate credit on depositing the sales voucher with the appropriate bank or finance house.
2. The funds are normally credited without recourse, thereby eliminating a guarantee of payment by telephone.
3. As an easy and trouble-free method of payment, it can attract a custom which might not otherwise have been forthcoming.
4. Mail and telephone order facilities may be available to the merchant. Retailers' own cards are also available.
5. The bulk of the administration is done centrally, and there is little or no necessity for extra resources to maintain accounts.
6. Normally only one VAT invoice is required each month for the commission.
7. Company credit cards are now available for directors and employees to meet their expenses for payment by direct debit. This scheme features personalised cards for the authorised company employee, produces a company statement, and narrative memoranda for each company employee. These are sent to the company monthly and give the company an average of 17 days' credit.
8. Both the supplier and the lender are liable to credit card users buying goods and/or services for £100 or more.

The credit card has many advantages

Costs of the credit card

1. There is normally a joining fee, paid only once.
2. There is a service charge on each transaction, which falls on the trader; it is normally between 3 and 5 per cent.
3. Be sure that the cost of accepting credit card transactions does not unacceptably reduce your mark-up (for example, on a single low-cost item with an already slender margin).
4. For company credit cards there are various conditions, including an overall credit limit.

Obtaining a credit card facility
1. Application to the issuing bank or finance house.

2. Visit by credit card consultant.
3. Completion of essential details on application form.
4. Acceptance.

What telecommunication equipment will you need?

Telephone
- Combined with answerphone and/or fax
- Portable phone you can carry from room to room
- Mobile phone you can use around the country
- Switchboard gives you several lines

Answerphone
Accepts calls while you are out. You can phone in and listen to any messages.

Fax
Enables you to send documents using a phone line, with immediate delivery. Can be used as a photocopier in an emergency, but the quality will not be good and the cost per copy will be high. A fax does not constitute a legal document, and some fade over time.

Mail services

Services offered by the Post Office

Can your business survive with the Royal Mail? In addition to the basic delivery service, the Post Office provides a range of additional services. Which of the following will help your business? Current prices are available in the 'Postal Rates' booklet. Contact the Post Office for further details.

Facility	Service	Notes
PO Box number	Collect or deliver letters and parcels	Provides earlier availability or correspondences
Business reply	1st or 2nd class mail	Application needs sample envelope
Freepost	1st or 2nd class mail	Usually for direct response sales campaigns
Recorded delivery	Signed delivery	Provides proof of delivery
Registered post	Insured, signed delivery	Mainly for valuables. First class mail only
Franking machines	Mailout franking	Rental or purchase agreed with manufacturer. Gives advertising and security benefits
Datapost	Same day collection and delivery between most UK business centres	Cash or credit. Also international up to 30 kg per item. Not for high value goods
Special delivery	Next day delivery	Excludes Channel Islands, Isle of Man, where Express Delivery Service applies
COD	Cash on delivery	Must be registered (letters or parcels)
Household delivery	Leaflet delivery to every letter box in area; targets may be specified as business or residential	
Parcels	Three-day service	Also local routes, max 30 kg. Size limits apply

Facility	Service	Notes
Direct mail Mail Sort	Same day posting	
Bulk rebate service	Delivery within seven days excluding weekends	Rebates on pre-sorted mailings over 4000 letters at one time, on a sliding scale from 15 to 30 per cent

◀ CHAPTER 9 ▶

EMPLOYMENT

Sources of employees

As an aid to finding the appropriatcly qualified person for employment, this list has been prepared:

Finding candidates for employment

- Existing employees
- Other businesses
- Relatives and friends
- Jobcentre
- Careers Office
- Placement Officers at schools and colleges
- Job advertisements – local press, radio/TV
- Recruitment and placement agencies
- Personnel managers handling a redundancy programme

Planning the employment interview

In view of the high costs to the business of poor recruitment, this list is a summary of the minimum essential preparation.

The interview and what is to be learned from it

Is there a *written* : Job description?
                  Personal profile?
What *must* you learn from the interview?

....

....

List the following:

Rates of pay – immediate – after training – overtime – bonuses, commissions
Hours of work/working week – breaks
Holidays
Other benefits – vehicle – health insurance – pension

Have you checked:

- How income tax will be deducted? ☐
- National Insurance? ☐
- Statutory Sick Pay? ☐
- Statutory Maternity Pay? ☐
- Equal Opportunities and similar legislation? ☐

Can the workplace be visited?

Who will make up the interviewing team?

....

....

Personal profile

The employment of the right person in a small business is vital. The table opposite may be used to assess prospective employees, partners, working directors, and even, to an extent, new shareholders.

This profile will help a business to remain with equal opportunities and sex discrimination legislation.

Does your application form help you to get this information?

Qualifications for employment		
	Required (= must have)	*Desirable (= nice to have)*
1. Age		
2. Education		
3. Training		
4. Experience		
5. Abilities/Skills		
6. Ambitions/Future		
7. Attitudes		
8. Health		
9. Location		

Employees' statutory rights

For employees working more than 16 hours per week and for those working between 8 and 16 hours per week, and subject to service of various lengths, there are statutory rights in respect of:

Statutory rights of employees

1. Written particulars of the terms of employment
2. Wage or salary pay statement
3. Notice of termination of employment
4. Time off for public duties
5. Provisions in connection with pregnancy, maternity and the right to return to work.
6. Guarantee payments
7. Payment when suspended on medical grounds
8. Redundancy
9. Dismissal
10. Statutory Maternity Pay (SMP)
11. Statutory Sick Pay (SSP)
12. The health and safety at work and anti-discrimination legislation applies to all employees.

Full details can be found in *Croner's Reference Book* and *An A–Z of Employment Law*, Peter Chandler (Kogan Page).

Taking on an employee

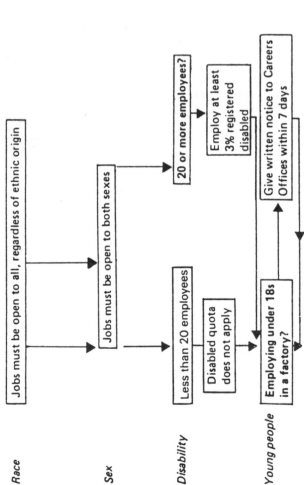

Race

Jobs must be open to all, regardless of ethnic origin

Exemptions. Genuine occupational qualifications, private households, training in skills to be used abroad, seamen recruited abroad, Northern Ireland. Some are likely to be removed, so check.

Sex

Jobs must be open to both sexes

Exemptions. Only if worker's sex can be shown to be a genuine occupational qualification, eg acting role, private households, communal accommodation.

Disability

20 or more employees?

Employ at least 3% registered disabled

Less than 20 employees

Disabled quota does not apply

Young people

Employing under 18s in a factory?

Give written notice to Careers Offices within 7 days

Consult Jobcentre if unable to do so

Notes

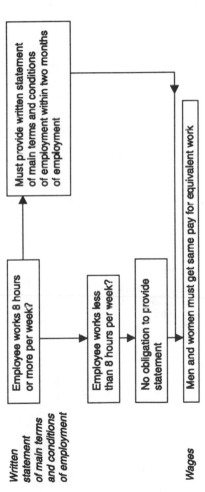

Written statement of main terms and conditions of employment

Employee works 8 hours or more per week?

Must provide written statement of main terms and conditions of employment within two months of employment

To include main terms and conditions, pay, holidays, details of notice and discipline procedures (seek help from ACAS).

Employee works less than 8 hours per week?

No obligation to provide statement

Wages

Men and women must get same pay for equivalent work

(Continued overleaf)

137

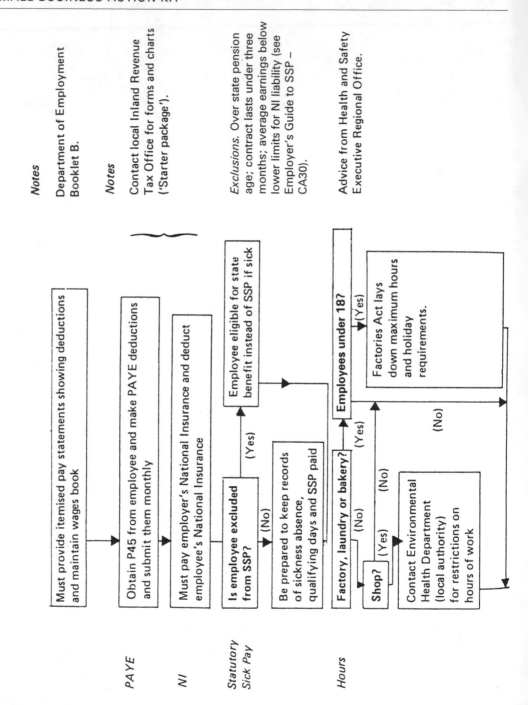

PAYE

Must provide itemised pay statements showing deductions and maintain wages book

Obtain P45 from employee and make PAYE deductions and submit them monthly

Notes

Department of Employment Booklet B.

Notes

Contact local Inland Revenue Tax Office for forms and charts ('Starter package').

NI

Must pay employer's National Insurance and deduct employee's National Insurance

Statutory Sick Pay

Is employee excluded from SSP? (Yes) / (No)

Employee eligible for state benefit instead of SSP if sick

Exclusions. Over state pension age; contract lasts under three months; average earnings below lower limits for NI liability (see Employer's Guide to SSP – CA30).

Be prepared to keep records of sickness absence, qualifying days and SSP paid

Hours

Employees under 18? (Yes)

Factory, laundry or bakery? (Yes) / (No)

Shop? (Yes) / (No)

Factories Act lays down maximum hours and holiday requirements.

Contact Environmental Health Department (local authority) for restrictions on hours of work

Advice from Health and Safety Executive Regional Office.

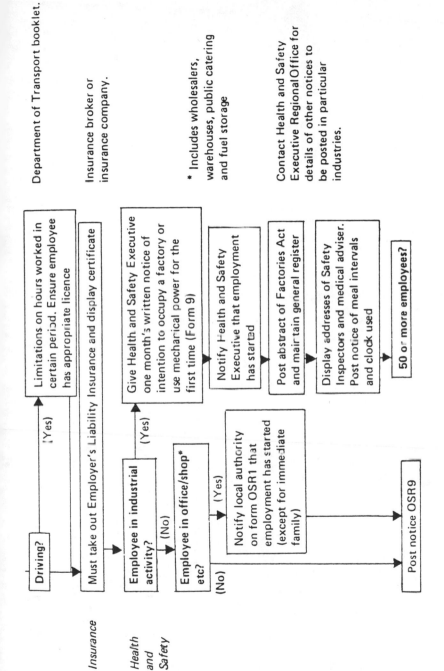

Department of Transport booklet.

Insurance broker or insurance company.

* Includes wholesalers, warehouses, public catering and fuel storage

Contact Health and Safety Executive Regional Office for details of other notices to be posted in particular industries.

Driving? — (Yes) — Limitations on hours worked in certain period. Ensure employee has appropriate licence

Insurance — Must take out Employer's Liability Insurance and display certificate

Health and Safety — Employee in industrial activity? — (Yes) — Give Health and Safety Executive one month's written notice of intention to occupy a factory or use mechanical power for the first time (Form 9) — Notify Health and Safety Executive that employment has started — Post abstract of Factories Act and maintain general register — Display addresses of Safety Inspectors and medical adviser. Post notice of meal intervals and clock used — 50 or more employees?

(No) — Employee in office/shop* etc? — (Yes) — Notify local authority on form OSR1 that employment has started (except for immediate family) — Post notice OSR9

(No)

139

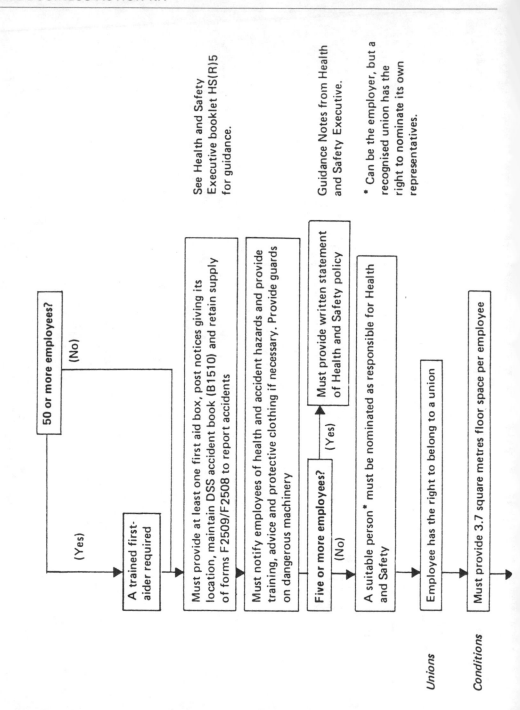

50 or more employees?

(Yes) (No)

A trained first-aider required

Must provide at least one first aid box, post notices giving its location, maintain DSS accident book (B1510) and retain supply of forms F2509/F2508 to report accidents

See Health and Safety Executive booklet HS(R)5 for guidance.

Must notify employees of health and accident hazards and provide training, advice and protective clothing if necessary. Provide guards on dangerous machinery

Five or more employees?

(Yes) (No)

Must provide written statement of Health and Safety policy

Guidance Notes from Health and Safety Executive.

A suitable person* must be nominated as responsible for Health and Safety

* Can be the employer, but a recognised union has the right to nominate its own representatives.

Unions

Employee has the right to belong to a union

Conditions

Must provide 3.7 square metres floor space per employee

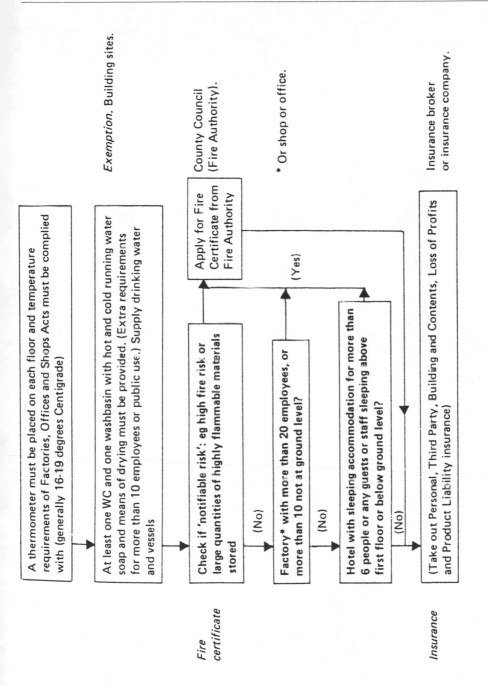

A thermometer must be placed on each floor and temperature requirements of Factories, Offices and Shops Acts must be complied with (generally 16-19 degrees Centigrade)

At least one WC and one washbasin with hot and cold running water soap and means of drying must be provided. (Extra requirements for more than 10 employees or public use.) Supply drinking water and vessels

Exemption. Building sites.

Fire certificate

Check if 'notifiable risk': eg high fire risk or large quantities of highly flammable materials stored

(No)

Factory* with more than 20 employees, or more than 10 not at ground level?

(No)

Hotel with sleeping accommodation for more than 6 people or any guests or staff sleeping above first floor or below ground level?

(No)

(Yes)

Apply for Fire Certificate from Fire Authority

County Council (Fire Authority).

* Or shop or office.

Insurance

(Take out Personal, Third Party, Building and Contents, Loss of Profits and Product Liability insurance)

Insurance broker or insurance company.

141

Pay As You Earn (PAYE) and National Insurance (NI)

Immediately, in the case of a limited company, and very early in the life of a sole trader, the business must act as a tax gather for the government. This flowchart shows the weekly, monthly and annual routines to be observed.

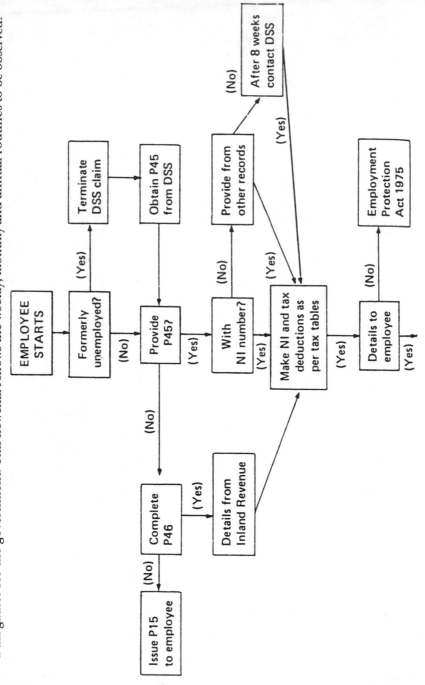

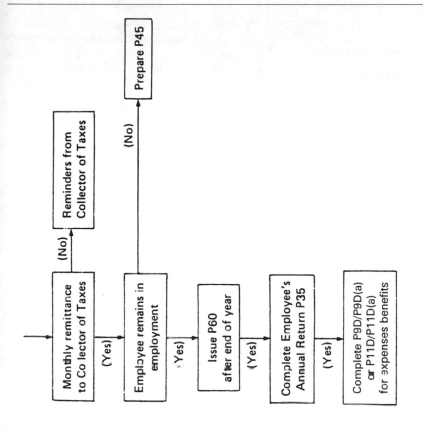

The business should have a legal adviser capable of providing guidance to ensure proper respect for employment law. The solicitor would also act for the business when an employee or former employee made claims arising from termination of employment or disciplinary action.

Additional reference

Employment Protection (Consolidation) Act 1978.

National Insurance payments

National Insurance All four classes of National Insurance contributions could affect the smaller business. These flow charts show how payments should be handled.

Class 1 contributions for employed persons

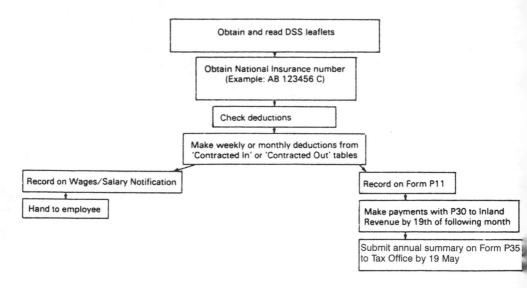

NB. Directors are also employees. Reduced contributions are payable by those who hold a Certificate of Election or a Certificate of Reduced Liability.

Class 2 contributions for self-employed persons

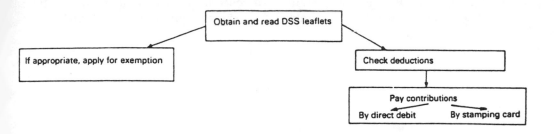

NB. Self-employed persons are *not* eligible for Unemployed Benefit, Industrial Injuries Benefit or earnings related benefits.

Class 3 contributions
Class 3 contributions are voluntary, and may be made by persons not gainfully employed in Great Britain. The fixed contribution may be paid by:

- Direct debit
- Stamping a card
- Lump sum payment at end of tax year.

Class 4 contributions for self-employed persons
Class 4 contributions are akin to an additional income tax. The contributions are collected by the Inland Revenue alongside Schedule D liabilities and relate to taxable profits between upper and lower limits.

Statutory Sick Pay (SSP)

Statutory Sick Pay

The SSP scheme has been in force since 6 April 1983. For those not familiar with its operation, their solicitor or accountant can help. These notes provide a brief introduction to the subject. Please see also leaflet CA30.

Employee	Employer	Notes
	Establishes notification rules and qualifying dates	
Goes sick		
Phones to	Nominated person	Appointed to note absence
	Logs in Absence record	Official record of absence, can be inspected by DSS. Contains other basic details of QUALIFYING DAYS PAYMENTS – to be kept for three years
Returns to work Completes ABSENCE STATEMENT Provides DOCTOR'S NOTE for absences above 7 days	Retains document(s)	
	Makes SSP payments Deducts SSP payments made from settlement with Inland Revenue (if applicable)*	Record on Form P11
	Annual summary	Use Form P14

* Check the rules in the SSP manual to see if you can recover the SSP you have paid.

Statutory Maternity Pay (SMP)

These notes provide a brief guide and your solicitor and accountant will give further help. Please see also leaflet CA29.

Employee	Employer	Notes
	Establishes notification rules and qualifying dates	
21 days before expected week of confinement (EWC), or as soon as practicable, informs and gives evidence of pregnancy in FORM MATB1 or doctor's certificate	Nominated person logs in absence record Make SMP payments starting any week from 11th to 6th week before EWC	Appointed to note absence
Chooses when pay to start Must give 21 days' written notice of intention to return to work	Retains documents Deducts SMP payments from settlements with Inland Revenue* Can require confirmation of return at least 49 days before EWC	Official record of payments can be inspected by DSS

* Check the rules in the SMP manual to see how much of the SMP you have paid you can recover.

Subcontractors' tax certificates

For some industries, notably the construction industry, there are benefits to both the contractor and the subcontractor if the latter holds a 714 certificate (Department of Employment).

1. *Start-up as an uncertified subcontractor.*

   Contractor deducts tax.
   Contractor pays deductions to Inland Revenue.
   Subcontractor registers as self-employed with local tax office.
   Inland Revenue makes adjustments after end of tax year.
   Subcontractor pays own Class 2 National Insurance contribution.
   Subcontractor signs off DSS benefits.

2. *Subcontractor applies for 714 certificate:* the authorities are unlikely to issue a 714 until some significant time after the start-up.

Subcontractor must be UK based in relevant industry.
Subcontractor must have good record of employment.
Subcontractor must have good record of tax and NI contribution payments.
Subcontractor must have proper business records and facilities.

3. *Certified subcontractor advises contractor*

Relieves contractor of administration.
Subcontractor issues 715 voucher for every payment.
Subcontractor maintains necessary records.
Subcontractor makes returns to Inspector of Taxes.

NB. The 714 Certificate exists in four forms:

For individuals 714I
For partnerships 714P
For certain companies 714C
For special situations 714S

The *contractor* has an obligation to check:

- Names and photographs on 714I, 714P, 714S
- Expiry date
- Identity of bearer

to avoid tax liability.

Health and safety at work: Checklist

Health and safety matters

Under the Health and Safety at Work Act 1974, the employer (even if he or she *is* self-employed) has major responsibilities which may be tested through these questions. Both your solicitor and the Health and Safety Executive can help with uncertainties.

The location

Access	Is it adequate?
Neighbours	Will they harm your staff (dust, smell, noise etc)
	Will you harm their staff (dust, smell, noise etc)

The premises

Space	Is it big enough?
Ventilation	Is it adequate?
Heating	Is it adequate?
Lighting	Is it adequate?
Electrical installation	Is it in good condition?
Fire precautions	Are escapes marked and assembly areas identified?
	Are fire extinguishers of correct type?
	Is the fire alarm fitted and tested?
Floors, stairs	Are they sound and non-slip?
Toilets	Are they in a satisfactory condition?
	Are there enough?
Safety audit	When was it last done?

Equipment

First aid	Have you got a first aid kit? Safety showers?
	Protective gear?
Machinery	Is it properly installed?
	Is it properly guarded?
Statutory inspections	Has a surveyor from your insurers examined your:
	– air receiver or compressor
	– steam boiler
	– lifting tackle
	– cranes
	– lifts
	– pressure vessels?

Materials handled

Toxic	Are precautions adequate?
	Effluents and waste disposal?
Inflammable*	Are precautions adequate?
	Flameproof equipment?
Corrosive	Are precautions adequate?
Dust/fume control	Is local exhaust ventilation required?
Protective clothing	Is any required? Is it issued and used?

* Flammable has the
same meaning, ie easily
set on fire.

Environment

Noise	Is your process very noisy?

What precautions do you need to take?

Systems of work

Methods of work   Are they carefully thought out?
                  Are they safe?

Training   Do your employees know what to do?
                  Have they been warned about potential risks
                  and the precautions to be taken?
                  What is the existing pattern of evacuation
                  drills?

Supervision   How do you make sure they work in
                  accordance with instructions?

Others

Safety   If you have more than five employees, you
                  must have a written safety policy.

Safety representatives   If you have a recognised trade union, they
                         may appoint safety representatives.

Notification of accidents   If a serious accident happens in your
                            premises, you must inform the relevant
                            authority as soon as possible.

The 1993 Management of Health and Safety at Work Regulations

1993 Management of Health and Safety Regulations

An important new set of (legally binding) health and safety regulations were introduced in 1993. To make sure that you comply with these requirements you must ensure that:

- A 'risk assessment' exercise has been undertaken to identify any possible dangers to the health and safety of employees or anyone else likely to be affected by the firm's operations;
- Someone devises a plan of implementing preventive and protective measures;
- Workers are given clear information about risks, in language they can understand;
- Employees are capable of avoiding risks;
- Equipment is suitable for its intended use and will only be used for appropriate purposes;
- Equipment is selected taking into account working conditions and the hazards of the workplace;

- Workers are given proper training and information in relation to the equipment they use;
- Unavoidable risks relating to handling operations are identified having regard to the shape, size and weight of the load, workplace conditions and the handler's posture while performing handling operations.

CHAPTER 10

ARE BIG PROBLEMS ON THE WAY?

Overtrading, a problem associated with success

Some problems arise from *success*. Difficulties may be caused by expanding the business more quickly than cash resources can stand. This is *overtrading*.

This checklist may help you to decide whether overtrading is a threat to your business.

Tick those which apply to your business

Customers clamouring for goods ☐

Stocks increasing ☐

Debits increasing ☐

Creditors crying out for payment ☐

Suppliers threatening to cut off supplies ☐

Overdraft limit breached: bank refusing to lend more ☐

For remedies, see opposite page.

The cash flow problem

Possible causes

Problems with cash flow

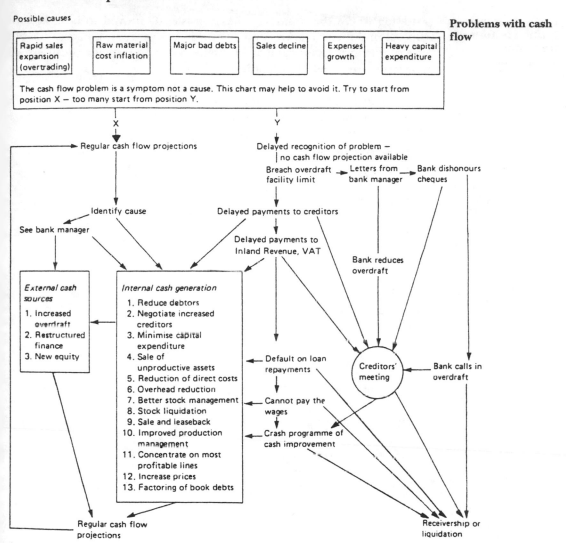

Take to the bank proof of what you have already done to improve the situation

Growth, survival or extinction?

Know where your business is: formats for control information

Knowing where the business is has consistently proved to be a key to survival in difficult markets and growth in buoyant ones. Pages 155–65 give simple formats for control information in typical smaller businesses. The items are set out in this order:

Responsibilities of the management
Sales and marketing effectiveness
Orders and shipments
Employment status
Cash

Liquidity
Debtors
Creditors

Profitability

Profit and loss account
Break-even

Assets

Balance sheet
Control ratios

Business planning

Cash flow projections
Financial planning
Management action plan

Responsibilities of the management

Who is responsible for:	To whom responsible?	Date of last report
Cash management		
Cash collection		
Costing		
Management information		
Accounts and bookkeeping		
Invoicing		
Sales		
Marketing		
Pricing		
Customer complaints		
Employee relations		
Recruitment		
Security		
Production		
– costs		
– quality		
– rate		
Purchasing		
Other key elements in the business		

Sales and marketing effectiveness

	Last month		Prior month		Year to date	
	Number	*Value of (monthly) business*	*Number*	*Value of (monthly) business*	*Number*	*Value of (monthly) business*
New accounts won						
Existing accounts lost						
Enquiries obtained						
Quotations put out						
Firm orders gained						
Firm orders as repeat business						
Tenders notified						
Tenders submitted						
Tenders awarded						
Market trends reported in national regional local } statistics						

ARE BIG PROBLEMS ON THE WAY?

Orders and shipments

Firm and despatchable orders on hand:

Volume _____ units

Value £ _____

	Orders completed			Orders booked for completion			
					Forward months		
	3 months ago	2 months ago	Last month	This month	2	3	4
High contribution products £							
Medium contribution products £							
Low contribution products £							
Total sales £							
Gross margin £							
Overheads £							
Gross margin – Overheads £							
Factory or business loading %							
Orders *not* despatched							
– supplier fault £							
– our fault £							

157

Employment status

	Last month	Prior month	Year to date
Desired number of employees			
Full time			
Part time			
TOTAL Full-time equivalents			
Employed at month end			
Vacancies unfilled			
Employees departed in month			
Resigned			
Dismissed			
Redundant			
Retired			
New employees recruited			
Absenteeism rate			

Cash

LIQUIDITY

	Now	Last week	Prior week	Last month
Cash in hand				
Balance per bank statement				
Payments drawn, not presented to bank				
Collections not credited to bank account				
Adjusted bank position				
Overdraft limit agreed with bank				

DEBTORS

	Last month	Prior month	Previous month
Total debtors (a)			
Moving annual sales + VAT (b)			
$\dfrac{\text{Debtors}}{\text{Sales}} = \dfrac{(a)}{(b)} \times 100$	%	%	%

In seasonal businesses, these percentages should be compared with figures from the corresponding period in past years.

CREDITORS

	Last month	Prior month	Previous month
Trade creditors (c)			
Moving annual trade purchases (d)			
$\dfrac{\text{Creditors}}{\text{Purchases}} = \dfrac{(c)}{(d)} \times 100$	%	%	%

In seasonal businesses, these percentages should be compared with figures from the corresponding period in past years.

Profitability

PROFIT AND LOSS ACCOUNT

	Current month				Financial Year to date			
	Last year	This year				Last year	This year	
	Actual	Actual	Budget			Actual	Actual	Budget	Variance
Sales									
Cost of sales									
Gross margin (B)									
Selling costs									
Distribution costs									
Administration costs									
Occupational costs									
Research and development costs									
Total overhead costs (A)									
Profit before interest and tax									
Interest									
Profit before tax									

BREAK-EVEN

Total overheads (A)
Gross margin % (B)
Break-even sales:

$$\frac{A}{B} \times 100$$

Assets

BALANCE SHEET

	Last financial year end	Last interim report	Current interim report
Fixed assets			
Land, buildings			
Fixtures, fittings and equipment			
Motor vehicles			
Total fixed assets			
Investments			
Current assets			
Stock			
Prepayments			
Debtors			
Bank			
Cash			
Total current assets			
Total assets			
Current liabilities			
Creditors – Trade			
– Others			
Accruals			
Overdraft			
Total current liabilities			
Long-term liabilities			
Proprietor's capital (net worth)			
Total liabilities and net worth			

CONTROL RATIOS

MAT is used below to stand for Moving Annual Total, ie, running 12-month figures.

	Last financial year end	Last interim report	Current interim report

Liquidity

$$\frac{\text{Current assets}}{\text{Current liabilities}}$$

$$\frac{\text{Current assets} - \text{Stock}}{\text{Current liabilities}}$$

Working capital

$$\frac{\text{Stock}}{\text{MAT cost of sales}}$$

$$\frac{\text{Debtors}}{\text{MAT sales}} \times 100\% \text{ (see page 161)}$$

$$\frac{\text{Creditors}}{\text{MAT purchases}} \times 100\% \text{ (see page 162)}$$

Financial structure

$$\frac{\text{Total liabilities}}{\text{Net worth}}$$

$$\frac{\text{MAT profit before interest and tax}}{\text{MAT interest paid}}$$

Profitability

$$\frac{\text{MAT profit before interest and tax}}{\text{Total assets}}$$

$$\frac{\text{MAT profit before interest and tax}}{\text{MAT sales}}$$

$$\frac{\text{MAT sales}}{\text{Total assets}}$$

163

Business planning
CASH FLOW PROJECTIONS

	This month	Month 2	3	4	5	6	etc
Opening balance (reconciled)							
Cash receipts							
Total inflow							
Cash payments							
Total outflow							
Closing balance							
Agreed bank overdraft facility							

FINANCIAL PLANNING

At the heart of business planning is forecast performance in these three areas:

	Current year by month	Next year by quarter	Following year
Cash flow (for format for first six months see above)	✓	✓	✓
Profit and loss account	✓	✓	✓
Balance sheet	✓	✓	✓

MANAGEMENT ACTION PLAN

Arising from the foregoing analyses, an action plan can be drawn up and assigned.

Major objectives*	To be done by	Completion date

* Clear and understandable
  Challenging but attainable
  Measurable
  Relevant
  Consistent with other objectives.

Heading for business ruin

Business failure runs at 80 per cent of all start-ups within their first five years. There are certain common causes of small business collapse. *Score your enterprise* by marking NIL where you are uncertain whether the item is clearly visible in your business. Where the item is clearly visible, score the points indicated. There are no *in between* scores.

Defects *If they are clearly visible in your enterprise, score the marks in the next column*		*Your score*
Management		
1. Autocratic boss who dominates his or her colleagues and takes no advice from them.	8	
2. The boss is also the chairman.	4	
3. Passive board of management not actively participating in decisions.	2	
4. Skills on the board are unbalanced, eg there are too many engineers	2	
5. No competent, strong-minded finance person guiding the business.	2	
6. Where relevant, no depth of management below the board.	1	
Accounting		
1. No budget (If there is, it is not compared with actual each month.)	3	
2. No cash flow plan (If there is, it is out of date.)	3	
3. No costing system: no one knows what each product really costs, nor its cash contribution to overheads.	3	
Response to change		
The enterprise exhibits some clear and vital example of failing to respond to change, eg: – An ageing product – Old-fashioned plant – Out-of-date marketing – Outmoded attitude to employees – Ageing management – No computer	15	
TOTAL FOR DEFECTS	43	

Mistakes _If they are clearly visible in your enterprise, score the marks in the next column_		Your score
Leverage The _capital gearing_ (external borrowing: proprietor's funds), or The _income grearing_ (profit before interest and tax: interest) of the enterprise is noticeably high.	15	
Overtrading Turnover is rising at a much faster rate than the finance available to fund it.	15	
Projects The enterprise has launched a project (eg building a factory, launching a new major product, guaranteeing a subsidiary company's loan) of such a size that if it goes wrong it will bring down the enterprise.	15	
TOTAL FOR MISTAKES	45	

Symptoms of failure _If they are clearly visible in your enterprise, score these marks_		Your score
Financial signs Control ratios are deteriorating and cash is becoming extremely scarce	4	
Creative accounting Accounts show evidence of window dressing to 'improve' profits, eg stocks valued higher, depreciation lower, repairs capitalised etc.	4	
Non-financial signs of distress Examples: Office needs painting, top management salaries frozen, capital expenditure decisions delayed, product quality or service deteriorating, morale failing	3	
Nose-dive Impossible to hide the last-gasp scramble for survival: writs, rumours, resignations.	1	
TOTAL FOR SYMPTOMS OF FAILURE	12	
GRAND TOTAL	100	

Is your score 25 or above?

If so, there are grounds for serious concern about the future of your business. _Now_ is the time to seek additional help. See your bank manager or accountant immediately.

Profit improvement

The five basic ways of improving profitability

The break-even chart on page 79 helps us to understand the five basic ways of improving profitability:

Key
Dotted line = projected figures
Unbroken = current figures

1. *Increase selling prices*

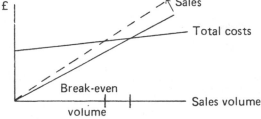

Increase prices with nil or acceptable decrease in sales volume to reduce the break-even volume – but see page 79.

2. *Reduce variable costs*

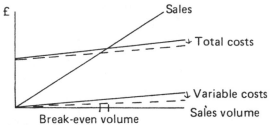

Reduce direct materials and/or direct labour costs to reduce variable costs. Thus total costs fall and reduce the break-even volume – see page 124.

3. *Reduce overheads (fixed costs)*

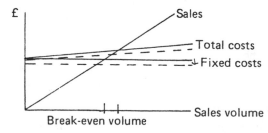

Reduce overheads to reduce total costs, in turn reducing the break-even volume – see page 124–5.

4. *Increase sales volume*

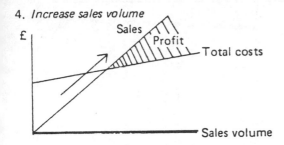

Move up the sales line by selling more without disturbing selling prices, fixed or variable costs. All sales above break-even volume yield a profit. Therefore, the higher the volume, the higher the profit if all the other items remain constant – see pages 55–61.

5. *Improve product mix*

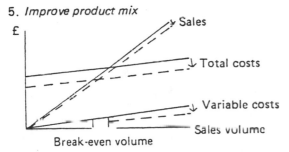

Concentrate on more profitable lines – often selling less in total – but also making correspondingly greater reductions in variable costs to reduce the break-even volume (see pages 45–6 and 79).

These are the only ways of increasing profitability.

The end

The biggest losses are incurred by 'pouring good money after bad'.

Sometimes the financial problem is one of cash where creditors cannot be paid, though asset values exceed all liabilities. Where the business is simply not paying its way early action is important to avoid debts running higher than necessary. Creditors will often wait for asset sales if they are kept informed of plans and progress by the proprietor. Full communication with creditors is essential.

At the very end, there are just a small number of options:

Limited company

Procedure	Instigated by	Requirements	Method
1. Voluntary Composition in satisfaction of debts or scheme of arrangement of affairs	Directors (unless company being wound up or subject to an administration order), approved by members and creditors	Solvency or insolvency, ie liabilities *including* contingent and prospective liabilities exceed assets	Directors nominate supervisor who reports to Court
2. Administration order	Members' and/or directors' and/or creditors' application for Court order	Potential or actual insolvency	Court appoints administrator
3. Administrative receivership	Creditor secured by floating charge	Breach of loan agreement	Administrative receiver appointed under terms of loan agreement
4. Receivership	Creditor secured by fixed charge	Breach of loan agreement	Receiver appointed under terms of loan agreement *or* by the Court
5. Application to Court for winding up Court order	Creditor and/or company, directors, supervisor, magistrates' court clerk, official receiver, Secretary of State		Liquidator appointed by the Court

Option 5 leads invariably to liquidation but options 1 to 4 do not, unless the company is insolvent.

Liquidation can be voluntary or compulsory and, where business failure looks increasingly likely, professional advice should be taken sufficiently early to safeguard the option for a members' voluntary liquidation (1 below).

Type of liquidation	Instigated by	Requirements	Method
1. Voluntary a. Members'	Resolution of 75 per cent of members	Solvency	Liquidator appointed by members
b. Creditors'	Ditto	Insolvency	Liquidator appointed by members or creditors
2. Compulsory (imposed by and in some cases supervised by the court)	Creditor and/or member, company, directors, supervisor, magistrates court clerk, official receiver, Secretary of State	Members' disputes, fraud or insolvency	Application to the court

The usual order of distribution of assets by the liquidator will be:

1. Debts secured by a fixed charge
2. Winding-up expenses
3. Preferential debtors, including:

   – business rate
   – UK taxes (contact your accountant)
   – six weeks' wages to a maximum of £184 per week
   – six weeks' accrued holiday remuneration
   – contributions payable under Social Security Acts and employment legislation
   – 12 months' PAYE deductions

4. Debts secured by a floating charge
5. Unsecured creditors
6. Deferred creditors
7. Shareholders

171

Partnership

Type of dissolution	Instigated by	Requirements	Method
1. (a) Arrangement or moratorium with creditors (b) Voluntary liquidation	Partners	Insolvency	Application to Court; partner's nominee is appointed supervisor and reports to court; may not result in bankruptcy
2. Forced	Usually a creditor	Insolvency	Court proceedings for recovery of money followed by a Court judgement and then appointment of a receiver or receiver and manager. And/or bankruptcy proceedings against one or more of the partners when personal assets in addition to business assets may be vulnerable
3. Selling the business	Partners	From choice, eg retirement, change of interests etc	Usually by sale of the business as a 'going concern' often including goodwill value

Partners are usually each responsible for *all* liabilities of the partnership as far as creditors are concerned. Internal sharing agreements do not affect this principle. Partnerships are best regulated by written agreement; otherwise the Partnership Act 1890 applies and some of the provisions are antiquated.

Sole trader

Procedure	Instigated by	Requirements	Method
1. Voluntary arrangement or moratorium with creditors	Proprietor	Insolvency	Proprietor applies to Court; his nominee is appointed supervisor and reports to the Court – may not result in bankruptcy
2. Forced	Usually a creditor, otherwise by the proprietor on realisation of insolvency	Insolvency	Receiver appointed by the court; may result in bankruptcy
3. Selling the business	Proprietor	From choice, eg retirement, change of interests etc	Usually by sale of the business as a 'going concern' often including goodwill value

The order of distribution of assets on liquidation follows the same pattern as in the winding-up of a company except that the unsecured creditors' and deferred creditors' claims are paid after those of the preferential debtors, as partnerships and sole traders cannot borrow under a floating charge. Last to be paid are the proprietors, and partners divide any balance after distribution in accordance with their initial contribution or the terms of their partnership agreement.

FURTHER READING FROM KOGAN PAGE

101 Ways to Start your Own Business, Christine Ingham

An A-Z of Employment Law, Peter Chandler

Be Your Own Accountant, Philip McNeill and Sarah Howarth

Be Your Own Boss!, David McMullan

Budgeting for Business, Leon Hopkins

Business Plans, Brian Finch

Buying a Shop, A St J Price

Buying Your First Franchise, Greg Clarke

Cash Flow and how to Improve it, Leon Hopkins

The Cheque's in the Post! Credit Control for the Small Business, Andrea Shavick

Customer Marketing, Jay Curry

Financial Management for the Small Business, Colin Barrow

Forming a Limited Company, Patricia Clayton

Getting Sales, Richard D Smith and Ginger Dick

A Handbook of Marketing and PR for the Small Business, Moi Ali

A Handbook of Personnel Management Practice, Michael Armstrong

How to Cut Costs in Business, John Allen

How to Prepare a Business Plan, Edward Blackwell

How to Run Your Own Restaurant, Bingley Sim and William Gleeson

How to Set Up and Run Your Own Business, Daily Telegraph Guide

How to Write a Staff Manual, Susan Brock and Sally Cabbell

Law for the Small Business, Patricia Clayton

The New How to Advertise, Kenneth Roman and Jane Maas

Ready-made Business Opportunities, Greg Clarke

Running Your Own Boarding Kennels 2nd edition, Sheila Zabawa

Running Your Own Catering Company, Judy Ridgeway

Running Your Own Mail Order Business, Malcolm Breckman

Running Your Own Market Stall, Dave J Hardwick

Running Your Own Photographic Business, John Rose and Linda Hankin

Running Your Own Pub, Elven Money

Running Your Own Shop, Roger Cox

Self Assessment for the Small Business and Self-Employed, Niki Chesworth

Starting a Successful Business, M J Morris

Successful Marketing for the Small Business, Dave Patten

Survive and Prosper, Toney Boffey

Taking up a Franchise, C Barrow and G Golzen (annual)

Taxes on Business, Kevin Armstrong

Understand your Accounts, A St J Price

Understanding Company Accounts, The Daily Telegraph Guide, Bob Rothenburg and John Newman

Working for Yourself, Godfrey Golzen (annual)

Your Bank : Make it Work for your Business, Iayn Clarke and Penelope Kimber

Your Home Office, Peter Chatterton

◀ INDEX ▶

References in italic indicate figures or tables.